To DAY

Nice To meet you
Lets Do the music VDO
soon

The **Authorities**

~ *Powerful Wisdom from Leaders in the Field* ~

778-892-2834

BERNARD H. DALZIEL
Award Winning Author

@gmail.com

E | B

S | I

Read Page 8

Publisher
Authorities Press
Markham, ON
Canada

Printed in the United States and Canada.

FOREWORD

Experts are to be admired for their knowledge, but they often remain unrecognized by the general public because they save their information and insights for paying customers and clients. There are many experts in a given field, but their impact is limited to the handful of people with whom they work.

Unlike experts, authorities share their knowledge and expertise far more broadly, so they make a big impact on the world. Authorities become known and admired as leading experts and, as such, typically do very well economically and professionally. Most authorities are also mature enough to know that part of the joy of monetary success is the accompanying moral and spiritual obligation to give back.

Many people want to learn and work with well-respected and generous authorities, but don't always know where to find them. They may be known to their peers, or within a specific community, but have not had the opportunity to reach a wider audience. At one time, they might have submitted a proposal to the For Dummies or Chicken Soup for the Soul series of books, but it's now almost impossible to get accepted as a new author in such branded book series.

It is more than fitting that Raymond Aaron, an internationally known and respected authority in his own right, would be the one to recognize the need for a new venue in which authorities could share their considerable knowledge with readers everywhere. As the only author ever to be included in both of the book series mentioned above, Raymond has had the opportunity to give back and he understands how crucial it is for authorities to have a platform from which to share their expertise.

I have known and worked with Raymond for a number of years and consider him a valued friend and talented coach. He knows how to spot talented and knowledgeable people and he desires to see them prosper. Over the years, success coaching and speaking engagements around the world have made it possible for Raymond to meet many of these talented authorities. He recognizes and relates to their passion and enthusiasm for what they do, as well as their desire to share what they know. He tells me that's why he created this new nonfiction branded book series, The Authorities.

Dr. Nido Qubein
President, High Point University

TABLE OF CONTENTS

INTRODUCTION

This book introduces you to *The Authorities* — individuals who have distinguished themselves in life and in business. Authorities make a big impact on the world. Authorities are leaders in their chosen fields. Authorities typically do very well financially, and are evolved enough to know that part of the joy of monetary success is the accompanying social, moral and spiritual obligation to give back.

Authorities are not just outstanding. They are also *known* to be outstanding.

This additional element begins to explain the difference between two strategic business and life concepts — one that seems great, but isn't, and the other that fills in the essential missing gap of the first.

The first concept is "the expert."

What is an expert? The real definition is …

EXPERT: *a person who knows stuff*

People who have attained a very senior academic degree (like a PhD or an MD) definitely know stuff. People who read voraciously and retain what they read definitely know stuff. Unfortunately, just because you know stuff does not mean that anyone respects the fact that you do. Even though some experts are successful, alas, most are not — because knowing stuff is not enough.

Well, then, what is the missing piece?

What the expert lacks, "the authority" has. The authority both knows stuff and is *known* to know stuff. So, more simply …

AUTHORITY: *a person who is known as an expert*

The difference is not subtle. The difference is not merely semantic. The difference is enormous.

When it comes to this subject, there are actually three categories in which people fall:

- People who don't know much and are unsuccessful in life and in business. Most people fall in this category.

- People who know stuff, but still don't leave much of a footprint in the world. There are a lot of people like this.

- Experts who are also *known* as experts become authorities and authorities are always wondrously successful. Authorities are able to contribute more to humanity through both their chosen work and their giving back.

This book is about the highest category, *The Authorities* — people who have reached the peak in their field and are known as such.

You will definitely know some of *The Authorities* in this book, especially since there are some world-famous ones. Others are just as exceptional, but you may not yet know about them. Let me introduce you to Bernard H. Dalziel, our featured author.

Is creating a budget frustrating for you? Are you tired of trying to reach your financial goals, but being stymied by all the confusing terms? In *How To Do I.O.A.L.: A Simple Financial Blueprint*, Bernard H. Dalziel lays out a financial blueprint that can help us all to better understand our finances. At the same time, Bernard shares stories from his challenges, and how he turned them into opportunities.

Part of his financial literacy transformation includes changing how he viewed his abilities regarding money, and then creating a simple formula to help others change how they think about their finances. Throughout this chapter, Mr. Dalziel lays out the I.O.A.L. blueprint, and gives you tips on how to meet your financial goals.

Additionally, in How to Do I.O.A.L., Bernard shares the importance of financial mentors to help you move forward. He also defines a blueprint and how critical it is to create a financial plan with action items for now and in the future.

His concept is so automatic that you can use it right away to change your mindset. From Income through Liabilities, Bernard explains it all in simple terms that can help you to make critical choices for your financial success.

To truly understand all the benefits of your financial blueprint, turn the page and open your mind to I.O.A.L.!

They are *The Authorities*. Learn from them. Connect with them. Let them uplift you. Learning from them and working with them is the secret ingredient for success which may well allow you to rise to the level of Authority soon.

To be considered for inclusion in a subsequent edition of *The Authorities*, register to attend a future event at www.aaron.com/events where you will be interviewed and considered.

How to Do I.O.A.L.

A Simple Financial Blueprint

BERNARD H. DALZIEL

The tried and true principles of saving and spending less seem to be the only financial literacy that most of us are exposed to. For so many of us, that means we are armed with little knowledge about one of the most important aspects of our lives, which is how to manage the money that we all need to function and enjoy the experiences that give meaning and depth to our lives.

Throughout this chapter, I am going to share the I.O.A.L. system, one that focuses on four key areas that are critical to building your wealth and helping you grow your net worth. Along the way, I am going to help you gain a better understanding of how to meet your financial goals and positively impact your future. Let's get started!

THE BEGINNING OF MY FINANCIAL EDUCATION

I love to help others help themselves by providing solutions that can help them double their income and triple their time off. When I started out, it wasn't easy for me. I had a hard time growing up. I was definitely considered a problem child. In fact, I probably spent more time in the hallway than I did in the classroom!

Yet, that was not time that I wasted. Instead, I used it to dream and stretch my imagination, growing and developing my EQ versus my IQ. Since I was out there already, I got to know everyone. To me, a stranger was just a friend that I hadn't met yet.

I was ready to quit school at age 12. Yet, there were moments and individuals that helped me during this academic struggle. I had a counselor who taught me a secret that helped me to learn the 9 multiplication tables in seventh grade. At that point, I was skipping school on a regular basis. I was hauled back to school by a truant officer and assigned to a counselor named Tom. He became my friend, and told me that if I was determined to leave school, there were certain basic things that I needed to know, such as reading, writing, and arithmetic.

That was when he found out that I didn't even know my 9 multiplication tables. He helped me fill out a job application with a short quiz on it. One part of the quiz was the 9 multiplication tables. I had to write the multiplication table from 1 to 9, put four triangles in a square, and then mail it in. As I did the multiplication table, I counted down (see the diagram). Then I put an X in the box. Now I decided to mail it myself, but being dyslexic, I wrote my name and address on the front, and the address I wanted to send it to on the back. I forgot to put a stamp on it, but I did remember to put it in the mailbox. A week later, I received the call to come in for an interview for the position of an office boy. More about that later.

Notice all the things I did wrong, yet how it all came together. By putting the address in the wrong spot, but forgetting the stamp, the letter was essentially returned to the place that I wanted it to go all along.

I also read the book Psycho-Cybernetics by Maxwell Maltz. He was a plastic surgeon who found that individuals were no happier after plastic surgery, simply because they had changed their outside, but not their inside, which included how they thought about themselves.

I made the decision to change how I viewed myself. No longer was I going to see myself as an academic failure, but as someone with unique gifts and talents that I could share with others. I decided to dedicate my life to helping others to help themselves by providing easy to understand information. One area in particular that I knew I could help was by creating a simple formula that gives people a way to create a written financial plan or blueprint. It was meant to help them change the way they think about their finances and give them an easy step-by-step process for financial freedom and independence.

If the elevator for success no longer works for you, then I want you to have the ability to take the stairs, one step at a time. Most people don't plan to fail, they just fail to plan.

Granted, I still had obstacles and challenges to face. I was dyslexic, which made school a trial, as I mentioned earlier. Then I started down a self-destructive path, one that led to alcohol, smoking, and drugs. It was a way of life that could have cost me mine. Still determined to follow this path of self-destruction, I lost my father at the age of 15. Now, I had to stop doing drugs because I had to step up and help my mother. It was time for me to grow up. My mother, Irene Richardson, is an impressive individual, one who raised her children with a sense of purpose and a desire to learn. Even to this day, she is active, and her routine could wear me out! She taught me that common sense is not that common these days. At the ripe age of 89 years old, she takes no pills, just nutritional supplements, and leads a water aerobics class 6 days a week. Her one day off is for God, and she knows that God answers all who take a knee.

As I got closer to 16, I realized that I needed to be a man. I stopped using drugs and got my driver's license. I also joined the swim team. I truly started to take control of my life and shape it to fit my vision, instead of allowing others' opinions of my capabilities define me. By 19, I had taken the exam for industrial first aid, and I became a first aid attendant and night watchman.

Then I took on an apprenticeship and became a distribution engineer in Vancouver. At that time, I was making $50,000 a year. It was a chance to party, and I did that until I was 37. That was when I met my mentor Raymond Aaron, through his Dr. Al Lowry course on investing in real estate. I also took a Thurston Wright course. My world was on a high. I cleaned myself up, mind, body, and soul. I took a year off to work on my personal relationship with my daughter. At the time, I was earning $5,000 a month.

That was when life threw up a huge obstacle. My marriage was ending. The divorce was difficult, draining me mentally, physically, emotionally, and especially financially. Suddenly a judge was telling me that half my monthly income ($2,500) needed to go to my soon-to-be ex-wife. I was in debt and going through the divorce from hell when I reconnected with Raymond Aaron.

I signed up for his monthly mentoring program using my credit card. I was adding more debt, but Raymond told me to give him two years and I would be able to change my life. I completed the mentoring program and I still have the certificate hanging on my wall. I completed my divorce and refinanced my debts to a comfortable level.

The next few years saw my life taking an amazing turn for the better. I met and married the love of my life and was able to help her raise her son and godson. Both of these young men went on to receive Master's degrees in their chosen fields. My daughter became an RN and now I am about to be a grandfather. My life is rich and full of blessings, but I realized that now was the best time to reach out to others and share a way to make a financial blueprint simple. My goal is to make complicated things simple, and help us all to achieve a life of peace in the process.

One of the things I credit with helping me to achieve this level of success in my life is that I took advantage of having mentors. Too often, we assume that our experiences make us the best guide to create the future we want. I learned that this is not the case. Robert Kiyosaki, author of *Rich Dad, Poor Dad,* also served as a mentor for me. His cash flow game, and explanation of how and why we work, helped me to make changes in my mindset. I also found mentors in Brian Tracy; Fred Synder, a radio personality on *Of Your Money*; and Ralph Hahmann, author of *Pension Paradigm*.

Clearly, mentors helped me to define goals, create timelines, and stay accountable. I want you to find financial success, and that starts with tapping into the wisdom and experiences of others. If you would like to speak with me about mentoring, contact me at www.BenardHD.com.

WHAT IS A BLUEPRINT?

A blueprint is a planning tool or document created to guide you in the process of building or creating your financial success. It can include your priorities, projects, budgets, and future planning. It can be revised, but serves as a guide to help you understand where you are in your financial journey. You can also make adjustments or fine-tune it on a daily, weekly, monthly, quarterly, or yearly basis. This is because various factors in your life can change. My divorce was one such event, but I am sure that you can think of many other examples.

You could win the lottery and be a millionaire, or you could lose everything that you own to a natural disaster. Heaven forbid, you could get into a car accident and sustain severe injuries or, worse, lose a family member to death.

The point is that, whether you recognize it or not, we all have a financial blueprint, from the homeless man on the corner to the wealthiest CEO. It might be a conscious or unconscious thing, but it does exist. Others have it written down. What I am about to teach you can be written out by a 7th grader. Many of us don't have money problems per se but have accumulated a lot of debt and expenses.

I believe that if we learned this strategy in 7th grade, it could create a shift in how we handle our finances, allowing us to avoid the large amount of debt that most individuals carry today. What a difference we could create for the next generation by teaching them about saving and investment wealth accumulation, the difference between good and bad debt, and more. The point is that what you are doing now is based on what you were taught in the past. Yet, that is not going to help you to create the future that you want. The past doesn't equal the future.

HOW DO YOU CREATE A FINANCIAL BLUEPRINT?

Throughout this chapter, I am going to give you the tools to create your financial blueprint. I just want you to remember that you are trying to keep things simple, so don't be afraid of having to make adjustments along the way. As Raymond Aaron says, just keep failing forward. The important thing is to just do it!

You are starting on a journey, and you need to draw the map that will help you to reach your final destination. The phrase to do expresses motion or moving in a specific direction towards a person, place, or thing. The point is that you have to take action. Right now, you have to get out a pen and a piece of paper. I want you to get everything out of your head. Start with creating four quadrants, as seen in the diagram.

Next, I need you to collect information together, so you know how much debt you have and how much income you have, such as income statements, investment income, etc. When you do your first financial blueprint, I want you to go low on income and high on expenses. As you do the math, you will be able to see whether you are cash flowing positively or negatively.

Most broke people go high on income and low on expenses, then they wonder why they are part of the 80% of Americans struggling financially. Now that you are reading this chapter and committed to changing your financial future, you are on the way to creating meaningful change in your life.

The definition of do is to perform an act or duty, to execute a piece of work, to accomplish something, or to complete or finish it. I want you to see this financial blueprint as a means to complete the action of understanding your finances, so that you can make informed decisions now to create a different future.

It is up to you to do the work. I am merely here to provide guidance and inspiration as you follow the directions to complete your financial blueprint.

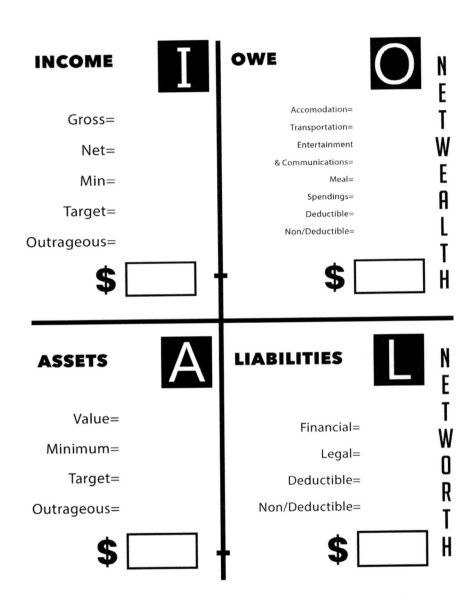

INCOME I OWE O N E T W E A L T H

Gross=

Net=

Min=

Target=

Outrageous=

$ ☐

Accomodation=

Transportation=

Entertainment
& Communications=

Meal=

Spendings=

Deductible=

Non/Deductible=

$ ☐

ASSETS A LIABILITIES L N E T W O R T H

Value=

Minimum=

Target=

Outrageous=

$ ☐

Financial=

Legal=

Deductible=

Non/Deductible=

$ ☐

I OWE AL

My uncle Al gave me a simple way to do a financial blueprint formula. He explained that what goes in must go out. It is like breathing. The body must take in oxygen, in order to expel carbon dioxide. The concept is so automatic for us that, without even thinking, all of us take regular and consistent breaths throughout the day. Here is what is interesting, however. When we take the time to do conscious breathing, where we mindfully concentrate on how we breathe, suddenly the whole tone of our breathing becomes different.

You get more out of it, and your mindset shifts. You sharpen your focus and it proves to be beneficial to bringing peace to your mind and body. There are many different ways of creating this focus, a sharpness of the mind. I can think of several, including yoga, stretching, meditation, and more. The point is that you are creating an internal focus that can help you to achieve anything that you set your mind to.

The formula is I.O.A.L., Income (I), Out of Wealth (O), Assets (A), and Liabilities (L). Each of these areas is part of what you need in order to create wealth and grow your net worth. I am going to cover each of these areas and help you to understand this formula and how you can use it to benefit your financial plans.

INCOME (I)

What is income? Strictly speaking, it is the money that you bring in, either through your job or investments. Consider this the way that you breathe in, drawing in the financial capital you need to pay for your lifestyle, including your basic needs and your wants. Another way to look at it is the money that an individual receives from a company in exchange for goods and services. You are exchanging your hours and skills for dollars. The reality is that your income is often capped by the number of hours you work in a day, the number of miles you can drive, or the number of customers you can serve.

Investing, on the other hand, brings in money but the exchange is not the same. The rich use money to invest and make more money, often while they are involved in other activities. Instead of exchanging their time and skills, they are providing capital, and that means their income truly can't be capped.

Most of us think of our income in terms of what we make in an hour, multiply it by the number of hours worked, and then do the math to come up with our annual income. Yet, the reality is that you don't make that much. The amount that you did all the math to come up with is just a gross number and doesn't reflect what you actually get to spend.

What you need to focus on instead is your net income. This income is essentially what you bring home after you pay taxes, health insurance, and any other deductions. You might find that, in the end, your annual salary based on your hourly wages is significantly higher than what you actually bring home on your paycheck. Why is this important to understand?

Simply put, many individuals make spending decisions based on what they make in gross income and then wonder why they are struggling to pay the bills or meet their financial goals. They are focused on the wrong number, and its negative impacts their ability to grow their net wealth. Let's start by determining what your net monthly income is. I want you to write down every source of income that you receive on a monthly basis before taxes and deductions. Once you have that number, you can then subtract your taxes and deductions to come up with your net monthly income.

Now that you know what that amount is, it is time to look at where that income goes. Remember, many individuals plan their expenses based on their gross income, which means that they are going to find themselves in the hole every month. How often do you find yourself struggling from paycheck to paycheck, barely getting by, let alone putting yourself in a position to save and invest?

I want you to understand that just by acknowledging that there is a difference between your gross and net income, you are already ahead of so many individuals who are exchanging hours and skills for dollars. This is because you see the potential to rid yourself of the cap that comes with exchanging hours for dollars, and see the possibilities to increase your income with no limits.

When you choose to invest, it needs to be from the head and not the heart. Too often, people fall for a great story, but a poor business plan. Don't be one of them!

Pick your investments with an eye to the bottom line. What is the business plan, and what types of capital do they need to achieve it? Do their financial statements reflect a good use of capital, or do they struggle to make ends meet?

Consider using the Rule of 72. Einstein, who believed that one of the wonders of the world was compounding interest, came up with the rule. He explained that if you divide 1 into 72, then you get 72. So, if an investment pays 1% of interest, then it will take you 72 years to double your money. Now if that same investment paid you 72% interest, then it would only take you one year to double your money.

Recognize that there are wealth killers. These are taxes and inflation.

Working with professionals, you can find ways to legitimately reduce your tax bill. Inflation, however, is not something that you can easily control. Therefore, in the Rule of 72, it is important to use a 3% percentage for inflation. Essentially, now you divide 3 into 72 and you come up with 24. That means in 24 years, the price of everything will have doubled. Therefore, when you are determining whether an investment is a good idea, you have to think about whether your return will be greater than the inflation during the same period. If not, then it is not going to help increase your wealth but may actually decrease it.

It is a question of finding the right type of investments that can work for you, based on your investment knowledge and risk tolerance.

Additionally, certain investments can create a greater tax liability based on the percentage of income earned. Therefore, you need to work with a tax professional to determine the best ways to legally minimize your tax bill through deductions. You may also choose to sell an investment to keep your income percentage lower and thus reduce your tax liabilities.

Many individuals argue about the amount of taxes they pay, or see them as excessive. I am not saying that those things might not be true, but at this point, governments depend on the tax revenue paid by their citizens. Here is a point that I thought was interesting from the New Testament of the Bible. Jesus was approached by the Pharisees and asked whether he should pay a temple tax. Now the Jews had no love for Roman taxes, and Jesus knew that their motive was to try to trip him up.

Instead, Jesus had one of his disciples pull out a coin and he asked whose face was on the coin. When the Pharisees responded that it was Caesar, Jesus responded, "Render therefore unto Caesar the things which are Caesar's, and unto God the things that are God's." The point? That taxes and the expenses associated with them are what we render to the government for the services it provides. At the same time, we can render receipts or other documentation to reduce what we owe, just as I am doing to have a $20,000 tax bill adjusted.

Therefore, whether you like it or not, these taxes are going to reduce your gross monthly income for years to come. However, there are ways to reclaim some of that money through your tax-deductible expenses. Working with a tax professional, you can find the best way to do so, recognizing that there are legal ways to effectively reduce your tax bill.

Another point to remember is that not all income is created equally. What do I mean by that? You have interest income, wage income, and rental income, for example. Each of those can result in a different tax rate, with different deductions that are applicable, as well as different rules for what must be reported. Recognize that you need to understand where your money is coming from to achieve the wealth goals that you want in your life.

Our next section is going to focus on Out of Wealth Expenses (OWE), which is where the income meets the expenses.

OUT OF WEALTH EXPENSES (OWE)

Your income is your wealth, and it provides you a means to pay for the things you need and want. These expenses typically reduce your wealth over the course of the month. When you think of this aspect of the blueprint, think of it as breathing out, expelling your financial capital in a variety of ways.

Take a moment and write down all of your monthly expenses. The list is going to include your mortgage or rent, utilities, car payment, insurance, internet, cell phone, and whatever else drains your income throughout the month. There are also those incidentals that you don't think about, because they have become automatic. Your stop at the coffee shop in the morning for that amazing latte? Out of wealth expense. Your regular lunch out with your workmates? Out of wealth expense. These little expenses can add up significantly over the course of a month. You might want to consider making note of every dollar you spend over the course of the week. You may be surprised at how much money simply disappears without you being consciously aware of it.

Remember **ATEMS**:

A – Accommodations

T – Transportation

E – Entertainment

M – Meals

S – Spending

Each of these has an impact on your budget. For instance, accommodations often take the largest chunk of your budget, with transportation next, then entertainment, communications, data, meals, and other spending. This type of spending could even include buying chocolate from a child for a fundraiser at school. Other expenses can include everything from lottery tickets to coffee and medical bills.

Now, there are other expenses that many of us deal with. Student loans, credit card debt, and perhaps even medical expenses. All of it adds up and can significantly reduce your income. There are ways to reduce those expenses, including refinancing loans for a lower interest rate or reducing your credit card spending. You also need to find ways to pay down debt faster, because this will save you money in the long run. What do I mean by that?

Most debts involve paying some form of interest on the debt. It is how the lenders make money from the individuals that they lend to. Now some interest rates are smaller than others, and obviously, the better your credit score the lower the interest rate is likely to be. Why? Because the higher credit scores are seen as lower risk to the lender, hence they receive the benefits in terms of lower interest payments.

However, when your credit score is lower, your interest is typically higher, and it costs you more to borrow money. The best way to save money on interest is to pay more than the minimum and apply as much as possible to the principal of the loan. Doing so will reduce the amount of interest paid over time. I have seen several examples of individuals who end up paying thousands of dollars in interest on their credit cards, simply because they refuse to make more than the minimum payments. Do not fall into this trap.

The best way to save money on interest is to negotiate a better rate, and always pay more than the minimum. When you are offered great credit offers, be sure to read the fine print. You may find that if you cannot pay the balance in full by the end of the term, you may be facing higher interest fees.

Once you pay down debt, it is important to keep it down. There are two types of debt: the type that is for non-assets and the debt for assets. The reason this difference is key is because, when you create debt to buy assets, you are building your net worth. When you grow non-asset debt, you are actually reducing your net worth and lowering your wealth.

If you have written all those expenses down, including food, gas, and what you spend on clothes, then you know what your out of wealth expenses are. Is that out of wealth number lower or higher than your net income? If it is higher, then you are in good shape and can start looking for ways to increase that income even further through investing.

However, if your net income is below your out of wealth expenses, then you are going to have to make some adjustments before you can start actively building wealth. The first step was already done when you listed all your expenses. Look over that list and don't make anything safe. Everything has the potential to be cut. For instance, those coffee shop visits? Perhaps they need to be on the chopping block to give you back more of your net income.

Anything that is an expense should be on this list, but keep in mind that choosing your expenses can mean you save money, or you might find that you are spending more than you need to in terms of taxes.

Look at your credit card debt. Are you getting your credit cards paid down, only to spend on them again, perhaps even drawing them over the limit regularly? All of these areas are places that you can start to reduce your out of wealth expenses. The point of this exercise is not to deprive you of the things that make life enjoyable, but to look for ways to make your net income and your out of wealth expenses balance. Eventually, the goal is to make sure that your out of wealth expenses are significantly lower than your net income.

One of the ways to do so is by tracking your expenses. If an expense is tax deductible, keep the receipt and then use that deduction when you file your taxes. To do this effectively, keep all your receipts and then separate them with your accountant into two piles, tax deductible and non-deductible. You might be surprised at how many deductions you have that you may have never claimed before.

Understand that money for business-related expenses is likely to be tax deductible, but personal items are not. Pay cash for personal items and then borrow for business expenses, thus allowing for the interest paid on business loans to be a tax deduction.

Think D=Deductible and ND=Not Deductible. Clearly, you can see the benefits of being a part-time business owner, even while you are an employee. Still, to be sure that you are getting all the tax benefits from your deductions and to determine which ones you qualify for, please consult with a tax professional.

Why do you think the rich become rich and stay that way? Because they tailor their lifestyle to a portion of their net income and then stick to it. They look for means to bring down their tax bill and do the recordkeeping necessary to achieve that. Additionally, they look for ways to increase that income, which leads me to Assets (A).

ASSETS (A)

To put it bluntly, assets are what you could sell to pay your debts. It could be your home, your car, or other valuables, such as jewelry. All of these items are assets. Your ability to purchase new assets can be based on your net income, but purchasing assets allows you to grow your net worth.

Investments can be a way to create assets. For instance, you might have $100,000 to invest. Now you could buy a rental property free and clear for that amount, or you could take that same amount and use it for down payments on four other properties. The result is that you have significantly increased your net worth by the value of those assets, but you have also increased your monthly net income due to the rental income.

Assets can be collateral for loans, or a way to get a lower interest rate. Home Equity Lines of Credit (HELOC) are a great way to maximize the asset you have in your home. You can pay the interest only or pay the whole amount off at any time. It allows you flexibility to invest in additional assets over time.

Assets are a critical part of building your wealth. I like to think of them as an acronym for the types of investments out there.

- **A** – Accumulating
- **S** – Several
- **S** - Stocks
- **E** – Estates
- **T** – Trusts
- **S** – Securities

Note that the point of accumulating these things is to create wealth, by the income they produce and the value they have against the debt that you might carry to purchase them. Choosing your investments wisely can help you to increase your assets and positively impact your net worth. Every investment has a level of risk, but the point is to balance your level of risk with the return from that investment.

In real estate, for example, you are focusing on being cash flowing on a property. That means the property covers its own expenses and still provides a positive income to you. I want you to remember that investments will have losses from time to time, but the point is that you don't want to have to continue to put income into an investment, because if it is not increasing in value, you are losing money.

I want you to get off your ass and do something to achieve something.

Are you willing to step outside of your comfort zone and try different investments? It might include spending assets to build your own business. The value of the business can grow, thus giving you an asset for your hard work.

I pointed this out because your ability to grow your income and purchase assets will be limited by your net income. When you work a traditional wage job, it caps your net income by the hours you work and the size of your paycheck. I am here to tell you that business ownership can mean taking your net income and growing it with no cap.

Now you might not be comfortable running a business, or you might be unsure of how certain things work when it comes to running a business. However, that is why you need to be willing to work with professionals. They can supply the knowledge and experience you lack. Plus, you don't want to be doing every job involved in running a business. You do not have enough time or energy to achieve all of that. The term is delegating, and it is key to any successful business.

Remember, you are doing something to achieve the wealth you want. Start looking at business opportunities with a critical eye. What is the investment needed, and the potential rate of return? How long before the business would be cash flowing? You might find, for example, that a franchise offers you the ability to purchase a business with all the systems in place, which may reduce your initial investment. However, franchises can also limit your ability to make changes as you see fit.

Therefore, it is important to weigh your options before choosing a business to invest in or purchase outright. Plus, when you purchase a business, you take on liabilities as well. However, liabilities are littered throughout the different types of assets available.

Let's move on to Liabilities (L) and how they can impact your wealth.

LIABILITIES (L)

Part of the point of liabilities is understanding that they are the items that reduce your net worth and negatively impact your wealth. Granted, they might be necessary expenses, but the point is that they are reducing the amount of net income you have to build your wealth.

You can think of them as sunk costs, ones that you are not likely to recoup as part of your investments and wealth building strategy. It could be insurance, setting up a trust or will, and consulting with professionals to determine the best tax strategy for your circumstances. The point is that these expenses are not going to be recovered, but the amount of these expenses also needs to be monitored. You might find yourself spending more than you should on sunk costs, and that can negatively impact your wealth.

However, the real liability is when you lie about your abilities, and you limit what you are capable of. So, you take advice from broke friends and family members, instead of consulting with those individuals who are professionals and experienced in generating wealth. Here is where I want to encourage you to look for mentors or coaches, and follow them.

They have experience and knowledge that you might not, but they also can help you to capitalize on the knowledge and experience that you already have. These mentors have walked the path that you are starting down, and can be critical to helping you achieve your goals and objectives. These are the individuals that can give you encouragement, and can also hold you accountable for achieving what is possible in your life.

CREATING TARGETS TO ACHIEVE YOUR VISION

When it comes to creating more income, you want to have several different targets. I think of them as the minimum, the medium, and the maximum. The minimum is essentially what you are making as a net income right now, factoring in wage increases or perhaps additional investment income. Now you might set your minimum as slightly higher, so you have a goal to shoot for in terms of increasing your net income from month to month.

The medium is a larger goal, outside of your comfort zone, that makes you have to hustle a bit to achieve it. You might take on an extra project for additional income beyond your job, or you might find yourself investing more. The point of medium is to make you stretch yourself further than you have before. To achieve your goals in terms of growing your wealth, you need to be willing to step outside of your comfort zone. Medium goals are meant to be a driver for that. At the same time, when you achieve a medium goal, you feel the rush that comes from accomplishing something and it pumps you up. Suddenly, you can see that more is possible. That is where the maximum comes in.

Now I have heard this goal referred to as outrageous, but the point is that this goal means you are really going to have to stretch yourself and take a gigantic leap outside of your comfort zone. It might even mean completely changing your lifestyle to break the barriers keeping you from reaching that maximum goal. From month to month, you are going to be able to reach plenty of minimum goals and even a few of the mediums, but you might think that the maximum goals are just too far out of reach.

I am here to tell you that is not the case. In fact, every time you reach a medium goal, you put that maximum goal closer and make it easier to reach. Even if you don't achieve it right away, you don't feel like a failure, because you achieved one of your other goals. The point is to put achievement on a sliding scale, making it easier to keep yourself pumped up to achieve the financial goals and dreams that you have always envisioned.

Part of this process involves changing how you think about building wealth. You want to use your income to generate future income. Your wealth is going to be tied to the investment choices you make and how you use those investments to essentially fund the purchase of future investments. If your investments have investments of their own and you are living off of that income, you are generating a consistent income stream that will positively impact your net wealth for years to come.

As an investor, you also have the opportunity to have your money start making money for you by using a professional. It is important to remember that there are individuals out there who spend their days working hard at finding the right investments to fit a variety of circumstances or investing goals. They are going to listen to your vision and help you make smart investment choices to achieve it.

Interview people and find the ones who are successful. For instance, if you decide to use a financial planner, ask how much they made last year. If it was less than you, then that is not the person you want working with you, because he is broke! You want to work with successful people to achieve your own success.

One of the key points I want you to understand from this chapter is that, as an employee, everyone is benefiting financially but you! Self-employed individuals pay the same tax rate as employed individuals, but they get to take deductions not available to employees, plus they have a more flexible schedule. Business owners get even more deductions and tax incentives. Optimize your income by owning a business. If you are thinking that owning a business is time-consuming and you don't have the time, consider hiring a general manager to run the business for you. For more information about the benefits of business ownership to your financial success, visit my website, www.transformationalblueprints.com.

Then you receive the benefits of owning the business, while being able to collect the income and still pursue what you enjoy in life.

Your circumstances can also change throughout your life, meaning that your financial vision is altered as well. Working with professionals can help you to keep your investments in line with your vision, even as it changes throughout your lifetime.

CREATING YOUR FINANCIAL BLUEPRINT

Finally, I want to discuss how this all can impact the life that you live. Many of us have dreams and goals, but the financial realities are limiting us from achieving them. I want you to be able to live the life you have always dreamed of, and fulfill your purpose. To do so, you need financial resources. When you choose to work with a financial professional, you get access to someone who can help you to achieve the financial resources necessary to achieve your dreams.

You have the ability to create an amazing life, but you have to believe that you are worth it. Once you make that conscious decision, then the next step is to define what amazing is to you. Everyone's idea of an amazing life is different, depending on their own personal experiences, beliefs, and values.

I want you to take a minute and define an amazing life for yourself. I can give you one example of how I value myself, and what I believe is a critical part of my amazing life. I always travel first class. Now, it is more expensive than a seat in economy or business class, but I value myself and see it as a priority not to spend hours cramped as I fly. Granted, this might not be one of your priorities, but that is what makes this part so interesting. All of us are unique, and so each of our lives can be amazing based on those unique aspects.

Get excited about the possibilities. Define your amazing life and then act to create it. If you wait for someone else to give it to you, you will be waiting a long time. My mother is still incredibly active, living life to the fullest. It is an example that inspires me to get the most out of every day of my life.

I also want to stress the importance of finding support to create real change in your financial life. After all, it isn't going to be easy to change how you view money, how you interact with it, and how you invest it. In fact, you might be so focused on just paying this month's bills that you can't even imagine life more than 30 days from now. That is the mentality that you need to break. It takes conscious effort to create that mental change, to shift your mindset.

After all, it took years to create the habits and mindset that are now your automatic default. When you change the default, it takes time to make it permanent. To be successful at it, you must get started. Financial shifts require effort as well, but they are so worth it. Do not be quick to assume that you can't do it! Instead, focus on the blueprint and your action steps in each area. Perhaps you just focus on one area at first, then shift to another. Over time, you will see the change, and its impact on your life.

Throughout this chapter, I have shared key strategies and important information that can help you through the process of creating wealth and growing your net worth. It comes down to a simple formula, one that requires you to think in terms of algebraic equations. (And you said that you would never use that again!)

Income – Out of Wealth Expenses = Your Net Wealth

Assets – Liabilities = Your Net Worth

These two points are essentially your financial blueprint. No matter what you do financially, it fits into one of these four categories. The point is to make smart choices that positively impact these areas and thus increase your financial wellbeing. Go to BernardI.O.A.L..com to find more information on how this financial blueprint can help you to achieve success.

What are some ways that you can make real change in these areas? Let's look at all of them one at a time.

- **Income** – Look for ways to increase your income through investments or business ownership. These options allow you to use your money to make more money, instead of just putting more hours in at a job. Remember, you can only work so many hours a week, which naturally limits how much income potential is available at a traditional job.

- **Out of Wealth Expense** – Choose your priorities and then work to manage your out of wealth expenses. Always remember to live within your net income, not your gross income!

- **Assets** – Building a portfolio of assets is key to growing your net worth. Choose your assets, not only for their current value, but for how those assets can grow over time. Work with a professional financial manager to help you invest effectively to increase your net worth and build income streams that allow you to live the life you want.

- **Liabilities** – Not all liabilities are the same. Some are the result of doing business, including insurance and legal or tax guidance. Limit liabilities that drain your resources unnecessarily.

Each of these areas is part of making your finances what you need them to be in order to achieve an amazing life. I have focused on your mindset, on your choices, and on ways you can create real change. However, they all require you to get up and move. You need to act, to embrace your abilities, and focus on what you are capable of.

Too many of us sell ourselves short and end our lives wondering what we missed out on, because we did not embrace our abilities and talents. Don't make that mistake!

Granted, you might not be interested in an investment because it doesn't mix with your values or it is not going to get you where you want to go in the timeframe you have already defined. The point is to explore the options and find the ones that work for you.

I met a wealthy friend who told me about a great book, Rich Dad Poor Dad by Robert Kiyosaki. That book opened my eyes to so many concepts that before had appeared complicated. It was as I read his book and took inspiration from it that I had a better understanding of income and how to generate it, as well as the tax implications of that. Today, I help people determine the best investments based on their goals, helping them to understand how each income presents different tax rates and more.

Now is the time to act. Don't put it off until tomorrow or some future date that will never come. Instead, open your mind to the possibilities.

Years ago, a friend interviewed for a position as an office boy. It was going well, until she asked for his email address and he explained that he didn't have one. She politely said they couldn't use him, and that was the end of the interview. Instead of allowing a fear of rejection and the accompanying dejection take hold, he decided to get active.

He had $10, so he went to a wholesale fruit distributor and bought a bag full of produce. He then sold it door to door. That day, he doubled his money and a new venture was born. It took time, but he went from walking to riding a bicycle to owning a truck and then a fleet of trucks. His hard work created a viable business. Now, he could have let that interview bring him down but, instead, he used it as inspiration to move forward. I want to provide that same inspiration to you. I want to help you act to create your vision. Don't let the rejection get you and keep you from fulfilling your dreams and goals!

Let's get started working together as a TEAM (Together Everyone Achieves More). Please contact me at my website, www.transformationalblueprints. com, to create real change in your financial life, and discovering the resources to fund the amazing life that you deserve! In this chapter, I have shared how to map out your financial plan, creating a You Are Here point in your life. Now I need you to transform this moment, getting rid of what no longer serves you by transforming your thoughts and feelings, essentially exhaling your negative thoughts and emotions.

Part of that process involves taking action. What do you want to be known for at the end of your life? Name three things. Now is the time to create and build, so use those three things as a platform to get started. Let them help you to craft your mission statement and the theme song of your life. You are in control of your mind's eye, your dreams, and your creativity. These are the tools that will allow you to reach your destination and leave a legacy behind for generations.

Practice conscious bio-breathing. Take a moment to think about what you love, and then hold that breath and truly experience your thoughts. Recognize that in that very moment, there are thousands of cells are being born in your body! All those cells with be filled with the energy and information captured in your DNA. Now exhale on the negativity in your life, including jealousy, visualizing the cells dying and leaving your body within the time it takes to exhale. It is all mind over matter. If you don't mind, then it don't matter!

Life is a journey of experiences, but you are the one who takes those experiences and crafts them into a truly amazing life, one that will be a legacy for others to follow for generations!

Please go to www.transformationalblueprints.com to download the I.O.A.L. chart and to get more information and details about Bernard H. Dalziel.

Step Into Greatness

LES BROWN

You have greatness within you. You can do more than you could ever imagine. The problem most people have is that they set a goal and then ask "how can I do it? I don't have the necessary skills or education or experience".

I know what that's like. I wasted 14 years on asking myself how I could be a motivational speaker. My mind focused on the negative—on the things that were in my way, rather than on the things that were not.

It's not what you don't have but what you think you need that keeps you from getting what you want from life. But, when the dream is big enough, the obstacles don't matter. You'll get there if you stay the course. Nothing can stop you but death itself.

Think about that last statement for a minute. There's nothing on this earth that can stop you from achieving what it is that you want. So, get out of your way, and quit sabotaging your dreams. Do everything in your power to make them happen—because you cannot fail!

They say the best way to die is with your loved ones gathered around your bed. But what if you were dying and it was the ideas you never acted upon, the gifts you never used and the dreams you never pursued, that were circled around your bed? Answer that question right now. Write down your answers. If you die this very moment what ideas, what gifts, what dreams will die with you?

Then say: I refuse to die an unlived life! You beat out 40 million sperm to get here, and you'll never have to face such odds again. Walk through the field of life and leave a trail behind.

One day, one of my rich friends brought my mother a new pair of shoes for me. Now, even though we weren't well off, I didn't want them; they were a size nine and I was a size nine and a half. My mother didn't listen and told my sister to go get some Vaseline, which she rubbed all over my feet. Then my mother had me put those shoes on, minding that I didn't scrunch down the heel. She had my sister run some water in the bathtub, and I was told to get in and walk around in the water. I said that my feet hurt. She just ignored me and asked about my day at school, how everything went and did I get into any fights? I knew what she was up to, that she was trying to distract me, so I said I had only gotten into three fights. After a while mother asked me if my feet still hurt. I admitted that the pain had indeed lessened. She kept me walking in that tub until I had a brand new pair of comfortable, size nine and a half shoes.

You see, once the leather in the shoes got wet, they stretched! And what you need to do is stretch a little. I believe that most people don't set high goals and miss them, but rather, they set lower goals and hit them and then they stay there, stuck on the side of the highway of life. When you're pursuing your greatness, you don't know what your limitations are, and you need to act like you don't have any. If you shoot for the moon and miss, you'll still be in the stars.

You also need coaching (a mentor). Why? There are times you, too, will find yourself parked on the side of the highway of life with no gas in the vehicle. What you need then is someone to stop and offer to pick up some gas down the road a ways and bring it back to you. That person is your coach. Yes, they are there for advice, but their main job is to help you through the difficulties that life throws at all of us.

Another reason for having a coach is that you can't see the picture when you're in the frame. In other words, he or she can often see where you are with a clarity and focus that's unavailable to you. They're not going to leave you parked along the road of life, nor are they going to allow you to be stuck in the moment like a photo in a frame.

And let's say you just can't see you're way forward. You don't believe it's possible. Sometimes you just have to believe in someone's belief in you. This could be your coach, a loved one or even a staunch friend. You need to hear them say you can do it, time and again. Because, after all, faith comes from hearing and hearing and hearing.

Look at it this way. Most people fail because of possibility blindness. They can't see what lies before them. There are always possibilities. Because of this, your dream is possible. You may fail often. In fact, I want you to say this: I will fail my way to success. Here is why.

I had a TV show that failed. I felt I had to go back to public speaking. I had failed, so I parked my car for ten years. Then I saw Dr. Wayne Dyer was still on PBS and I decided to call them. They said they would love to work with me and asked where I had been. I wasn't as good as I had been ten years before, as I was out of practice, but I still had to get back in the game. I was determined to drive on empty.

Listen to recordings, go to seminars, challenge yourself, and you'll begin to step into your greatness, you'll begin to fill yourself with the energy you need to climb to ever greater heights. Most people never attend a seminar. They won't invest money in books or audio programs. You put yourself in the top 5 percent just by making a different choice than the average person. This is called contrary thinking. It's a concept taken from the financial industry. One considers choosing the exact opposite behaviour of the average person as a way to get better than average results. You don't have to make the contrarian choice, but if you don't have anything to lose by going that road, why not consider the option?

Make your move before you're ready. Walk by faith not by sight and make sure you're happy doing it. If you can't be happy, what else is there? Helen Keller said, "Life is short, eat the dessert first."

What is faith? Many of us think of God when we think of faith. A different viewpoint claims that faith is a firm belief in something for which there is no proof. I would rather think of faith as something that is believed especially with strong conviction. It is this last definition I am referring to when I say walk by faith not by sight. Be happy and go forth with strong conviction that you are destined for greatness.

An important step on your way to greatness is to take the time to detoxify. You've got to look at the people in your life. What are they doing for you? Are they setting a pace that you can follow? If not, whose pace have you adjusted to? If you're the smartest in your group, find a new group.

Are the people in your life pulling you down or lifting you up? You know what to do, right? Banish the negative and stay with the positive; it's that simple. Dr. Norman Vincent Peale once said (when I was in the audience), "You are special. You have greatness within you, and you can do more than you could ever possibly imagine."

He overrode the inner conversations in my mind and reached the heart of me. He set me on fire. This is yet another reason for seeking out the help of a coach or mentor or other new people in your life. They can do what Dr. Peale did for me. They can set your passion free.

How important is it to have the right kind of person/people on your side? There was a study done that determined it takes 16 people saying you can do something to overcome one person who says you can't do something. That's right, one negative, unsupportive person can wipe out the work of 16 other supportive people. The message can't be any clearer than that.

Let's face the cold, hard truth: most people stay in park along the highway of life. They never feel the passion, the love for their fellow man, or for the work they do. They are stuck in the proverbial rut. What's the reason? There are many reasons, but only one common factor: fear — fear of change, fear of failure, fear of success, fear they may not be good enough, fear of competition, even fear of rejection.

"Rejection is a myth," says Jack Canfield, co-author of The Chicken Soup for the Soul series. "It's not like you get a slap in the face each time you are rejected." Why not take every "no" you receive as a vitamin, and every time you take one know you are another step closer to success.

You will win if you don't quit. Even a broken clock is right twice a day.

Professional baseball players, on average, get on base just three times out of every ten times they face the opposing pitcher. Even superstars fail half of the time they appear at the plate.

Top commissioned salespeople face similar odds. They make may make one sale from every three people they see, but it will have taken them between 75 and 100 telephone calls to make the 15 appointments they need to close their five sales for the week. And these are statistics for the elite. Most salespeople never reach these kinds of numbers.

People don't spend their lives working for just one company anymore. This means you must build up a set of skills and experiences that are portable. This can be done a number of ways, but my favourite approaches follow.

You must be willing to do the things others won't do in order to have tomorrow the things that others don't have. Provide more service than you get paid for. Set some high standards for yourself.

Begin each day with your most difficult task. The rest of the day will seem more enjoyable and a whole lot easier.

Someone needs help with a problem? Be the solution to that problem.

Also, find those tasks that are being consistently ignored and do them. You'll be surprised by the results. An acquaintance of mine used this approach at a number of entry-level positions and each time he quickly ended up being offered a position in management.

You must increase your energy. Kick it up a notch. We are spirits having a physical existence; let your spirit shine. Quit frittering away your energy. Use it to move you closer to the achievement of your dreams. Refuse to spend it on non-productive activities.

What do people say about you when you leave a room? Are you willing to take responsibility—to walk your talk. There is a terrible epidemic sweeping our nation, and it is the refusal to take responsibility for one's actions. Consider that at some point in any situation there will have been a moment where you could have done something to change the outcome. To that end you are responsible for what happened. It's a hard thing to accept, but it's true.

Life's hard. It was hard when I was told I had cancer. I had sunken into despair, and was hiding away in my study when my son came in. My son asked me if I was going to die. What could I do? I told him I was going to fight, even though I was scared. I also told him that I needed some help. Not because I was weak but because I wanted to stay strong. Keep asking until you get help. Don't stop until you get it.

A setback is the setup for a comeback. A setback is simply a misstep on the long road of success. It means nothing in the larger scheme of things. And, surprisingly, it sets you up for your next win. It tends to focus you and your energy on your immediate goals, paving the way for your next sprint, for your comeback.

It's worth it. Your dreams are worth the sacrifices you'll have to make to achieve them. Find five reasons that will make your dreams worth it for you. Say to yourself, I refuse to live an unlived life.

If you are casual about your dreams, you'll end up a casualty. You must be passionate about your dreams, living and breathing them throughout your days. You've got to be hungry! People who are hungry refuse to take no for an answer. Make NO your vitamin. Be unstoppable. Be hungry.

Let me give you an example of what I mean by hungry ...

I decided I wanted to become a disc jockey, so I went down to the local radio station and asked the manager, Mr. Milton "Butterball" Smith, if he had a job available for a disc jockey. He said he did not. The next day I went back, and Mr. Smith asked "Weren't you here yesterday?" I explained that I was just checking to see if anyone was sick or had died. He responded by telling me not to come back again. Day three, I went back again—with the same story. Mr. Smith told me to get out of there. I came back the fourth day and gave Mr. Smith my story one more time. He was so beside himself that he told me to get him a cup of coffee. I said, "Yes, sir!" That's how I became the errand boy.

While working as an errand boy at the station, I took every opportunity to hang out with the deejays and to observe them working. After I had taught myself how to run the control room, it was just a matter of biding my time.

Then one day an opportunity presented itself. One of the disc jockeys by the name of Rockin' Roger was drinking heavily while he was on the air. It was a Saturday afternoon. And there I was, the only one there.

I watched him through the control-room window. I walked back and forth in front of that window like a cat watching a mouse, saying "Drink, Rock, Drink!" I was young. I was ready. And I was hungry.

Pretty soon, the phone rang. It was the station manager. He said, "Les, this is Mr. Klein."

I said, "Yes, I know."

He said, "Rock can't finish his program."

I said, "Yes sir, I know."

He said, "Would you call one of the other disc jockeys to fill in?"

I said, "Yes sir, I sure will, sir."

And when he hung up, I said, "Now he must think I'm crazy." I called up my mama and my girlfriend, Cassandra, and I told them, "Ya'll go out on the front porch and turn up the radio, I'M ABOUT TO COME ON THE AIR!"

I waited 15 or 20 minutes and called the station manager back. I said, "Mr. Klein, I can't find NOBODY!"

He said, "Young boy, do you know how to work the controls?"

I said, "Yes, sir."

He said, "Go in there, but don't say anything. Hear me?"

I said, "Yes, sir."

I couldn't wait to get old Rock out of the way. I went in there, took my seat behind that turntable, flipped on the microphone and let 'er rip.

"Look out, this is me, LB., triple P. Les Brown your platter-playin' papa. There were none before me and there will be none after me, therefore that makes me the one and only. Young and single and love to mingle, certified, bona fide and indubitably qualified to bring you satisfaction and a whole lot of action. Look out baby, I'm your LOVE man."

I WAS HUNGRY!

During my adult life I've been a deejay, a radio station manager, a Democrat in the Ohio Legislature, a minister, a TV personality, an author and a public speaker, but I've always looked after what I valued most—my mother. What I want for her is one of my dreams, one of my goals.

My life has been a true testament to the power of positive thinking and the infinite human potential. I was born in an abandoned building on a floor in Liberty City, a low-income section of Miami, Florida, and adopted at six weeks of age by Mrs. Mamie Brown, a 38-year-old single woman, cafeteria cook and domestic worker. She had very little education or financial means, but a very big heart and the desire to care for myself and my twin brother. I call myself Mrs. Mamie Brown's Baby Boy and I say that all that I am and all that I ever hoped to be, I owe to my mother.

My determination and persistence in searching for ways to help my mother overcome poverty and developing my philosophy to do whatever it takes to achieve success led me to become a distinguished authority on harnessing human potential and success. That philosophy is best expressed by the following …

"If you want a thing bad enough to go out and fight for it,
to work day and night for it,
to give up your time, your peace and your sleep for it…
if all that you dream and scheme is about it,
and life seems useless and worthless without it…
if you gladly sweat for it and fret for it and plan for it
and lose all your terror of the opposition for it…
if you simply go after that thing you want
with all of your capacity, strength and sagacity,
faith, hope and confidence and stern pertinacity…
if neither cold, poverty, famine, nor gout,
sickness nor pain, of body and brain,
can keep you away from the thing that you want…
if dogged and grim you beseech and beset it,
with the help of God, you will get it!"

The 3 Things You Need to Become a Real Estate Millionaire

The Right Way to Invest Successfully

RAYMOND AARON

I t seems like everywhere you look, someone is claiming that they became a millionaire by investing in real estate, and encouraging you to do the same. There are lots of TV shows about flipping houses for a fast buck that make it appear as if it's easy to find the right property and just as easy to sell it in a matter of months for a good profit. Unfortunately, that's not really how it works.

Investing in real estate is a proven way to make money, a lot of it. You could end up with millions, but you could also make a lot of very costly mistakes along the way. There has been so much hype about how easy it is to become a real estate millionaire that many people jump into the market without knowing what they are doing, and that's a shame, especially because qualified help is available.

Anyone can invest successfully in real estate if they have three things: a great real estate mentor, a proven real estate system, and a way to correctly predict the future. In other words, you need someone smart and knowledgeable to guide you, an understanding of the financial and legal aspects of buying, holding and selling real estate, and an ability to see societal trends and visualize how those trends will impact the real estate market.

A GREAT REAL ESTATE MENTOR

Investing on your own can be financially dangerous, especially for a first-timer. You're dealing with a lot of money, so any mistake can be a huge one. Buying at the wrong time in the cycle can kill your investments. And, regardless of the real estate strategy you employ, you're bound to hold onto properties for some period of time which means that severe negative cash flow and vacancies can ruin you. Plus, bad property management and a failure to know the most recent real estate and tax laws can get you sued.

An experienced mentor can help you choose the best real estate strategies for your situation, and the right properties in which to invest. They can also help you avoid the many possible pitfalls and make money while holding properties, and counsel you on when to sell for a great profit. Working with the right mentor can also keep real estate investing from becoming your full-time job.

Many people find that some part of the investment process is uncomfortable for them, whether it's initiating a conversation with a realtor, submitting an offer or hiring a property manager. A mentor can be very helpful in such situations as well.

In sum, learning from and working with the right mentor can make you a highly profitable investor in a relatively short period of time. Look for someone with years of experience and a proven track record.

A PROVEN SYSTEM

There's much more to investing in real estate than "buy low, sell high." To be successful, you must have the correct facts and the correct monthly habits concerning your real estate. Overall, you need to know what to buy, when to buy it, whether there will be a positive cash flow while you're holding on to it, and when to sell. Plus, what is the right low? What is the right high? How much money do you have to put down and how much income must be generated while you're waiting to sell?

Determining if a property is a good buy takes a lot of research and analysis. You will need to look at comparable purchase prices in the area, as well as rental fees. You'll also need to consider the location, the age and condition of the building, tax rates and about 30 other pieces of data. Evaluating the information for just one property could take you a day or more.

If you're serious about becoming a real estate investor, you are going to be considering quite a lot of properties on a regular basis. Even if you want to make investing your day job, you'll never have the time necessary to research fully and evaluate every property that comes to your attention. Hence, the first part of your system has to involve weeding out the lesser opportunities and focusing on the ones with potential.

The investors I mentor learn how to determine if a property is really a great deal in seconds. You only need two pieces of data: the purchase price and the current rent rate. Compare the two using a two-part formula. First, divide the asking price (outgoing funds) by 100. Then, given that current mortgage interest rates are below 8-10% divide the number you got by two. If the current monthly rent doesn't meet or better that second number, eliminate the property from consideration.

As an example, say the asking price is $1 million. If you divide it by 100, it comes out to $10 thousand. Divide again, by two, and you get $5 thousand. If the monthly rent isn't $5 thousand or more, you should pass on the property. You may miss out on a few winners using this system but, if you eliminate more properties than you think you should, you'll be successful and safe. Remember that, if interest rates rise significantly, you will need to adjust the formula to compensate.

Once you've weeded out the chaff from the wheat, do your due diligence on the remaining properties. Work closely with your mentor during this part of the process and, again, when it comes to making deals, say no more than you say yes. Just don't get cold feet or shy away from a great deal.

In terms of timing, it all comes down to momentum. There is always an overall upward momentum. Real estate prices go up and down, on an upwards track. So, one good profit strategy is to buy low, watch values rise and sell during the next boom. More precisely, you want to buy just as prices rise off the bottom (so that they're already rising) and sell when prices hit double the bottom, which is typically the very minimum prices rise to at the peak of the ensuing boom.

Don't attempt to predict the extremes — you will make a significant amount of money more safely buying just after prices begin rising (not the lowest point) and selling towards the end of the up period —without the risk associated with waiting too long and missing the highest point.

You'll also need a system for monitoring your investments while holding on until it's time to sell. Having a strong property manager is essential. So is reviewing rents taken in versus uncollectibles, repairs, and other expenses to ensure that your cash flow remains positive.

PREDICTING THE FUTURE

Good real estate investors learn to identify marketplace trends and buyers' or renters' needs. Start by investigating and tracking growth trends by neighborhood: are prices rising, is an area getting ready for a renaissance, are there new job opportunities nearby or is the area close to another neighborhood that's gotten too pricey?

Great real estate investors, however, go far beyond those basics. They look for large demographic or social elements that might provide the next big opportunity. The huge number of returning veterans after World War II led to a Baby Boom that provides the perfect example. Every stage of their lives brought an opportunity for marketers, real estate builders, and other manufacturers to fill unmet needs, be it starter homes for when they had children, tricycles for those children who were too young to ride a bike, or new sizes and types of cars. All of this was predictable, but no one noticed. Opportunities were capitalized upon as they arose, but imagine what financial success could have been attained if someone had predicted the Baby Boomers' needs in advance.

And, now, those Boomers are driving the growth of retirement communities and nursing homes. But, they are a more independent lot than their parents were, and have strived to remain young and healthy as long as possible. Quite a few of them can still live and thrive on their own, but many may need a little help at this point in their lives. They don't need or want an aide, nurse or social worker on a full-time basis and certainly aren't ready for a nursing home. That means there is a huge need for more up-to-date, internet-ready independent supportive living arrangements, of which there are too few. Investing in one now is bound to be a win.

Don't forget that those Baby Boomers had children of their own, and that created a mini baby boom. Think about the ways in which those children, now middle-aged adults, are different from their parents and what needs they might have, especially regarding real estate. You might also consider whether changes in the workforce, higher divorce rates and the economics of leaving home after college have implications for the real estate market as well. Keep your eyes and minds open!

If you would like to learn more about winning strategies for investing in real estate, please visit http://rarestmonthlymentor.com.

Happiness: How to Experience the "Real Deals"

MARCI SHIMOFF

I was 41 years old, stretched out on a lounge chair by my pool and reflecting on my life. I had achieved all that I thought I needed to be happy.

You see, when I was a child, I thought there would be five main things that would ensure that I'd be happy: a successful career helping people, a loving husband, a comfortable home, a great body, and a wonderful circle of friends. After years of study, hard work, and a few "lucky breaks," I finally had them all. (Okay, so my body didn't quite look like Halle Berry's—but four out of five isn't bad!) You think I'd have been on the top of the world.

But surprisingly I wasn't. I felt an emptiness inside that the outer successes of life couldn't fill. I was also afraid that if I lost any of those things, I might be miserable. Sadly, I knew I wasn't alone in feeling this way.

While happiness is the one thing we all truly want, so few people really experience the deep and lasting fulfillment that fills our soul. Why aren't we finding it?

Because, in the words of the old country western song, we're looking for happiness in "all the wrong places."

Looking around, I saw that the happiest people I knew weren't the most successful and famous. Some were married, some were single. Some had lots of money, and some didn't have a dime. Some of them even had health challenges. From where I stood, there seemed to be no rhyme or reason to what made people happy. The obvious question became: *Could a person actually be happy for no reason?*

I had to find out.

So I threw myself into the study of happiness. I interviewed scores of scientists, as well as 100 unconditionally happy people. (I call them the Happy 100.) I delved into the research from the burgeoning field of positive psychology, the study of the positive traits that enable people to enjoy meaningful, fulfilling, and happy lives.

What I found changed my life. To share this knowledge with others, I wrote a book called *Happy for No Reason: 7 Steps to Being Happy from the Inside Out.*

One day, as I sat down to compile my findings, all the pieces of the puzzle fell into place. I had a simple, but profound "a-ha"—there's a continuum of happiness:

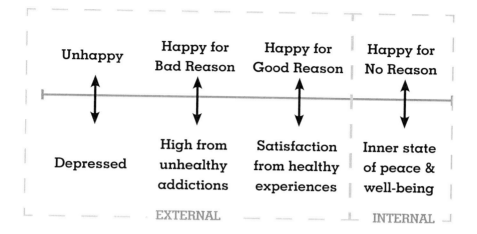

Unhappy	Happy for Bad Reason	Happy for Good Reason	Happy for No Reason
Depressed	High from unhealthy addictions	Satisfaction from healthy experiences	Inner state of peace & well-being
	EXTERNAL		INTERNAL

Unhappy: We all know what this means: life seems flat. Some of the signs are anxiety, fatigue, feeling blue or low—your "garden-variety" unhappiness. This isn't the same as clinical depression, which is characterized by deep despair and hopelessness that dramatically interferes with your ability to live a normal life, and for which professional help is absolutely necessary.

Happy for Bad Reason: When people are unhappy, they often try to make themselves feel better by indulging in addictions or behaviors that may feel good in the moment but are ultimately detrimental. They seek the highs that come from drugs, alcohol, excessive sex, "retail therapy," compulsive gambling, over-eating, and too much television-watching, to name a few. This kind of "happiness" is hardly happiness at all. It is only a temporary way to numb or escape our unhappiness through fleeting experiences of pleasure.

Happy for Good Reason: This is what people usually mean by happiness: having good relationships with our family and friends, success in our careers, financial security, a nice house or car, or using our talents and strengths well. It's the pleasure we derive from having the healthy things in our lives that we want.

Don't get me wrong. I'm all for this kind of happiness! It's just that it's only half the story. Being Happy for Good Reason depends on the external conditions of our lives—these conditions change or are lost, our happiness usually goes too. Relying solely on this type of happiness is where a lot of our fear is stemming from these days. We're afraid the things we think we need to be happy may be slipping from our grasp.

Deep inside, I think we all know that life isn't meant to be about getting by, numbing our pain, or having everything "under control." True happiness doesn't come from merely collecting an assortment of happy experiences. At our core, we know there's something more than this.

There is. It's the next level on the happiness continuum—Happy for No Reason.

Happy for No Reason: This is true happiness—a state of peace and well-being that isn't dependent on external circumstances.

Happy for No Reason isn't elation, euphoria, mood spikes, or peak experiences that don't last. It doesn't mean grinning like a fool 24/7 or experiencing a superficial high. Happy for No Reason isn't an emotion. In fact, when you are Happy for No Reason, you can have *any* emotion—including sadness, fear, anger or hurt—but you still experience that underlying state of peace and well-being.

When you're Happy for No Reason, you *bring* happiness to your outer experiences rather than trying to *extract* happiness from them. You don't need to manipulate the world around you to try to make yourself happy. You live from happiness, rather than *for* happiness.

This is a revolutionary concept. Most of us focus on being Happy for Good Reason, stringing together as many happy experiences as we can, like beads in a necklace, to create a happy life. We have to spend a lot of time and energy trying to find just the right beads so we can have a "happy necklace".

Being Happy for No Reason, in our necklace analogy, is like having a happy string. No matter what beads we put on our necklace—good, bad or indifferent—our inner experience, which is the string that runs through them all, is happy, and creates a happy life.

Happy for No Reason is a state that's been spoken of in virtually all spiritual and religious traditions throughout history. The concept is universal. In Buddhism, it is called causeless joy; in Christianity, the kingdom of Heaven within; and in Judaism it is called *ashrei*, an inner sense of holiness and health. In Islam it is called *falah*, happiness and well-being; and in Hinduism it is called *ananda*, or pure bliss. Some traditions refer to it as an enlightened or awakened state.

So how can you be Happy for No Reason?

Science is verifying the way. Researchers in the field of positive psychology have found that we each have a "happiness set-point," that determines our level of happiness. No matter what happens, whether it's something as exhilarating as winning the lottery or as challenging as a horrible accident, most people eventually return to their original happiness level. Like your weight set-point, which keeps the scale hovering around the same number, your happiness set-point will remain the same **unless you make a concerted effort to change it.** In the same way you'd crank up the thermostat to get comfortable on a chilly day, you actually have the power to reprogram your happiness set-point to a higher level of peace and well-being. The secret lies in practicing the habits of happiness.

Some books and programs will tell you that you can simply decide to be happy. They say just make up your mind to be happy—and you will be.

I don't agree.

You can't just decide to be happy, any more than you can decide to be fit or to be a great piano virtuoso and expect instant mastery. You can, however, decide to take the necessary steps, like exercising or taking piano lessons—and by practicing those skills, you can get in shape or give recitals. In the same way, you can become Happy for No Reason through practicing the habits of happy people.

All of your habitual thoughts and behaviors in the past have created specific neural pathways in the wiring in your brain, like grooves in a record. When we think or behave a certain way over and over, the neural pathway is strengthened and the groove becomes deeper—the way a well-traveled route through a field eventually becomes a clear-cut path. Unhappy people tend to have more negative neural pathways. This is why you can't just ignore the realities of your brain's wiring and *decide* to be happy! To raise your level of happiness, you have to create new grooves.

Scientists used to think that once a person reached adulthood, the brain was fairly well "set in stone" and there wasn't much you could do to change it. But new research is revealing exciting information about the brain's neuroplasticity: when you think, feel and act in different ways, the brain changes and actually rewires itself. You aren't doomed to the same negative neural pathways for your whole life. Leading brain researcher Dr. Richard Davidson, of the University of Wisconsin says, "Based on what we know of the plasticity of the brain, we can think of things like happiness and compassion as skills that are no different from learning to play a musical instrument or tennis …. it is possible to train our brains to be happy."

While a few of the Happy 100 I interviewed were born happy, most of them learned to be happy by practicing habits that supported their happiness. That means wherever you are on the happiness continuum, it's entirely in your power to raise your happiness level.

In the course of my research, I uncovered 21 core happiness habits that anyone can use to become happier and stay that way. You can find all 21 happiness habits at www.HappyForNoReason.com

Here are a few tips to get you started:

1. **Incline Your Mind Toward Joy.** Have you noticed that your mind tends to register the negative events in your life more than the positive? If you get ten compliments in a day and one criticism, what do you remember? For most people, it's the criticism. Scientists call this our "negativity bias" — our primitive survival wiring that causes us to pay more attention to the negative than the positive. To reverse this bias, get into the daily habit of consciously registering the positive around you: the sun on your skin, the taste of a favorite food, a smile or kind word from a co-worker or friend. Once you notice something positive, take a moment to savor it deeply and feel it; make it more than just a mental observation. Spend 20 seconds soaking up the happiness you feel.

2. **Let Love Lead.** One way to power up your heart's flow is by sending loving kindness to your friends and family, as well as strangers you pass on the street. Next time you're waiting for the elevator at work, stuck in a line at the store or caught up in traffic, send a silent wish to the people you see for their happiness, well-being, and health. Simply wishing others well switches on the "pump" in your own heart that generates love and creates a strong current of happiness.

3. **Lighten Your Load.** To make a habit of letting go of worries and negative thoughts, start by letting go on the physical level. Cultural anthropologist Angeles Arrien recommends giving or throwing away 27 items a day for nine days. This deceptively simple practice will help you break attachments that no longer serve you.

4. **Make Your Cells Happy.** Your brain contains a veritable pharmacopeia of natural happiness-enhancing neurochemicals — endorphins, serotonin, oxytocin, and dopamine — just waiting to be released to every organ and cell in your body. The way that you eat, move, rest, and even your facial expression can shift the balance of your body's feel-good-chemicals, or "Joy Juice", in your favor. To dispense some extra Joy Juice — smile. Scientists have discovered that smiling decreases stress hormones and boosts happiness chemicals, which increase the body's T-cells, reduce pain, and enhance relaxation. You may not feel like it, but smiling — even artificially to begin with — starts the ball rolling and will turn into a real smile in short order.

5. **Hang with the Happy.** We catch the emotions of those around us just like we catch their colds — it's called emotional contagion. So it's important to make wise choices about the company you keep. Create appropriate boundaries with emotional bullies and "happiness vampires" who suck the life out of you. Develop your happiness "dream team" — a mastermind or support group you meet with regularly to keep you steady on the path of raising your happiness.

"Happily ever after" isn't just for fairytales or for only the lucky few. Imagine experiencing inner peace and well-being as the backdrop for everything else in your life. When you're Happy for No Reason, it's not that your life always looks perfect — it's that, however it looks, you'll still be happy!

By Marci Shimoff. Based on the New York Times bestseller *Happy for No Reason: 7 Steps to Being Happy from the Inside Out*, which offers a revolutionary approach to experiencing deep and lasting happiness. The woman's face of the *Chicken Soup for the Soul* series and a featured teacher in *The Secret*, Marci is an authority on success, happiness, and the law of attraction. To order *Happy for No Reason* and receive free bonus gifts, go to www.happyfornoreason.com/mybook.

Investment Success and Successful Beliefs

JASON G. CHAN

"Why are you chuckling to yourself?" my brother asked as we passed by an upscale restaurant one night. "Did I miss something?"

"No, not really," I replied. "Remember those two Ferraris that were waiting for valet parking back by the restaurant that almost everybody who passed by, including us, were looking at and admiring? I just realized that if I wanted to, I could buy both of those Ferraris with cash, one for you and one for me."

Of course, I never did that. But that moment stuck in my head because it was the first time I realized that, financially, I had done okay for myself. I made my first million dollars investing in the stock market when I was just shy of 30 years old. My second million came shortly after that. That's when I stopped counting. I stopped counting because I finally found some comfort in knowing that my family was doing okay and that I was doing okay.

A few years before that, my father had suddenly passed away. It happened in 2008 in the middle of one of the greatest recessions in history. My family was entrenched in debt and my parents hardly had any retirement savings, let alone other investments. My two younger brothers and I were burdened knee-deep in student loan debt. I was living in my parents' living room because the basement where I had been living got flooded and became too moldy to stay in.

For most of my adolescent and early adult life, our family cash flow was tight, and we couldn't even afford a decent study desk. I haven't done too shabby for a boy whose desk was actually nothing more than a door flipped sideways and propped up by four poles on each corner; definitely not too shabby as an investor for someone whose degree was in fine arts and graphic design. I don't have a degree in business, finance or economics. I don't believe we need fancy degrees or education to do well in finance and investments or in life. For those who likes degrees, later in life I was told that I actually got a PhD earlier in life, since I was Poor, Hungry and Driven. At the end of the day, it's not your degrees or titles that make you, it's really about your vision and your beliefs.

YOUR BELIEFS ARE IMPORTANT

Sometimes people ask me what I did or what I invested in, hoping to get some insight as to how they too can achieve what I have. They're usually asking about specific things I did, specific things I invested in, or tools I used. What they don't understand is that these things are not the important part. Belief is where it all starts. To achieve investment success by having the proper successful beliefs, mental concepts, and proper mindset is the key.

After all, we all act and behave in certain ways because of our beliefs. Some beliefs serve us, some limit or deter us, and some set us astray. They shape what we do and how we do it. Before anything even starts, our beliefs tell us what we can do because they shape what we think is possible and what is not. Therefore, having the proper beliefs, or shaping what you already have, is really important in life, and also in investments. My purpose and goal is to help you adopt proper, empowering beliefs and realign, even discard, the negative ones as they relate to investments. It is only with a proper mindset and a successful beliefs system that you can get ahead in finances and achieve sustainable, consistent and long term investment success.

The first and, perhaps, the most important belief I want to share with you is it's possible for you to achieve financial and investment success. Not only can you achieve it, but you can achieve it on your own by empowering yourself to take control of your finances and investments. If a poor boy who started off living in a basement with a door as a study desk, who studied fine arts and graphic design, and who had large student loans and family debt could do it, so could you.

"It's Possible" is one of my favorite phrases from Les Brown. He goes on to describe that one of the keys to changing our belief system and enabling us to act on our dreams is knowing that something is possible. To know that a goal or that dream or that something we want or achieve has already been done or achieved by someone else, is to know that something is possible and achievable. More importantly, that "It's Possible" for you to achieve it too!

UNDERSTANDING FINANCE AND INVESTMENTS IS A LIFE SKILL

One of the first questions people come across when it comes to their finances and investments is, "Should I manage them myself or should I get someone else in the financial industry, such as an investment firm or bank, to manage them for me?"

Not only am I an individual investor who manages my own finances, I have also worked in the financial services industry, for one of the largest financial institutions in the country, as an investment sales representative for over 10 years. I am also a certified life coach who specializes in finance and investments. Through my various experiences, my short answer is that you should eventually invest in yourself and invest for yourself. Being able to take control and take charge of your finances and investments is a very liberating feeling that everyone should enjoy.

The investment service industry has a purpose and a place in everybody's life, but by no means should it be used or regarded as a long-term solution. It's like riding a bicycle with training wheels. Many people dream of financial freedom, but they are often dependent on an investment company to get them there. How could you be free and dependent at the same time?

Understanding finance and investments is a necessity in life. Just like eating and cooking, it's something we have to do for the rest of our lives. For this reason, I believe it's a life skill we should all acquire and develop. We have to deal with money, so we need to understand finance. Unless we spend every dime we earn or put everything under a mattress, we all have to invest. At the end of the day, nobody cares more about your financial future and well-being more than you.

HAVING SOMEONE ELSE MANAGE YOUR MONEY IS MORE COSTLY THAN YOU THINK

When it comes to eating, we won't eat out every meal, every day for the rest of our lives. We won't do that because we know it doesn't make sense and it gets expensive. So why would it make sense to pay someone else or a company to manage your investments every day for the rest of your life? Well, many people actually do that. One of the main reasons is because the investment industry has presented their fees in a way that seems deceivingly small and inexpensive. That's why many people don't mind "dining out" their whole lives.

Let's use the mutual fund industry as an example. The mutual fund industry is what most people are exposed to and familiar with when it comes to professional investment management. Aside from possible front-load and back-load fees and commissions, all mutual funds charge what they call a management expense ratio or MER. The MER alone for the average mutual fund ranges from approximately 2% - 2.5% a year. We'll take the low end of 2% to give them the benefit of the doubt. A 2% annual fee sounds small and nominal, doesn't it? The financial industry usually does not take the time or effort to explain what this fee actually means. Often customers are left with the impression that they get charged 2% MER from the gains that the company makes for them, if any.

In reality, that 2% MER is calculated and charged based on the entire amount of money they are managing for the customer, or what they call assets under management. What that means is, if you give them $100 to invest, they will charge you 2% on that $100, so essentially $2. Say you have $100,000 invested with them. At 2% MER, that works out to be $2,000 a year. For those who wish to have $1,000,000 ($1 Million dollars) a 2% MER would cost them $20,000 a year! To look at it from another perspective, a 2% MER fee in 5 years alone, works out to 10% (2% x 5). In 10 years, that works out to be 20% (2% x 10). In a mere 5 years and 10 years respectively, you would have paid out 10% and 20% of your hard-earned money in MER fees. Now consider that most people save and invest for retirement for about 35 years, how does the math work out for a long duration like that?

As I mentioned, the financial and investment industry is a business. Just like the restaurant industry and eating out, there is a time and place for services like that. However, it should not be used as a long-term solution, because it becomes very costly in the long run. I feel a true investment company and professional should be promoting financial freedom and independence, not financial dependence. Understanding finance and investments is truly a life skill that we should all acquire and develop. We can't afford not to.

In the examples above, I purposely kept the math simple and to the point and avoided financial jargon, such as compounding, time value, etc., because those are the kind of things that deter from the basic idea and confuse clients. The investment industry will critique our example and try to say that they will grow the client's money through the years. However, at the end of day, they cannot guarantee you any gains. So we won't factor that in. And to be fair, I won't assume they'll lose your money either. I kept it neutral in my example— no gains, no losses—similar to the "lost decade" that we experienced in the stock markets not too long ago.

INVESTING IS LIKE TREASURE HUNTING

When most people think of the world of investments and finance it seems overwhelmingly complex. A simple and interesting analogy I use to compare the world of investing and the investment industry is a big treasure hunt. If we were to look at it from this perspective, we would get a better understanding of how things work, many things would become apparent and begin to make sense.

So off to treasure hunting we go. Imagine we are in a world where treasure hunting is a big deal and almost everybody is out to find some treasure. Opinions on how to find treasure are a dime a dozen and everybody has their ideas and opinions.

Yet, despite the abundance of ideas and strategies floating around, many of these ideas tend to be passed around by people who have never found any significant treasure themselves. They hear and get these ideas and concepts from family members, a friend, a friend of a friend, and various media outlets. And where did many of these ideas originate from? A lot of these ideas actually came about through the "treasure hunting industry."

Yes, treasure hunting is such a big deal, there's actually a treasure hunting industry which is supposedly there to help you and guide you to find treasure. There are big corporate institutions with many employees who sell you treasure maps, treasure guides, strategies, tools and gadgets along with various products and services which they claim will help you find treasure. Many of them offer packaged plans to help treasure hunt for you through their professional and experienced treasure hunters.

The deal is that you put up all the capital to be used for the treasure hunt, but they do not guarantee you any success. The only guarantee is that they will charge you a management fee whether or not they find you treasure. And if they do end up finding treasure, they actually take a bigger cut of your money. So you put up all the money and take all the risk and they take a risk free payment from you in order to help you treasure hunt. And there are no guarantees of success. It's a pretty good business model for them, but not such a good business idea for you.

At some point you might begin to wonder that if these companies and their staff are so good at treasure hunting, how come they just don't focus on that and treasure hunt for themselves? Eventually, you'll realize that these companies actually make money from selling treasure hunting packages and products and by providing treasure hunting services. They don't make their money from actually finding treasure, per se.

Their frontline staff, sales representatives and professional treasure hunters, can give you all sorts of treasure hunting advice, ideas, and strategies, along with various treasure products and services the company has to offer. However, like most regular people, most of them have never found success in treasure hunting. The majority of their income actually comes from working their sales jobs and earning commission selling treasure hunting packages, products and services.

Sometimes you see some of these sales people enjoying the luxuries of life which can create the impression that they have actually found treasure from treasure hunting, but the reality is, they were actually just a successful sales person, not a successful treasure hunter.

Remember how we said that much of the common investment advice that floats around in public originated from these treasure hunting companies in the treasure hunting industry? A lot of the time this supposed treasure hunting advice is actually based on half-truths that are either outdated, have lost effectiveness, or have never been useful at all. They are mainly ideas and strategies used to promote and sell various treasure hunting packages, products and services.

There are actually really good and skillful treasure hunters out there. As you would expect, most of them spend their time treasure hunting for themselves. Some do open up treasure hunting companies to help others find treasure, but they usually require clients with lots of money and many of them have reached capacity and have stopped taking on new clients.

Keep this treasure hunting analogy in mind the next time you think about investments and the investment industry. It should give you an idea of how to make sense of it all and help you decide if you really wish to have someone else treasure hunt for you or not.

THE INVESTMENT LANDSCAPE HAS CHANGED

Since the new millennium, the stock market and investment landscape has been a lot different than it was in previous decades. This is not just a belief—it is a fact. It is important that we recognize and acknowledge this reality and incorporate it into our belief system for two main reasons.

First of all, in order to invest successfully and navigate through the stock market, we need to understand what kind of landscape and environment we are currently in. Imagine you are taking a road trip, how could you expect a to get from point A to point B if you were using an old and dated road map from many decades ago? I am sure it would be a frustrating trip with a few wrong turns here and there.

Secondly, understanding how the stock market and investment landscape used to be can help us understand where many investment ideas and strategies we still hear and read about came to be. More important is why they have lost relevance, effectiveness and significance.

Using the beginning of the new millennium, the year 2000, as a benchmark for the midpoint year of reference, let us take a look at the last 36 years of the S&P500, a popular and widely followed North American stock index. We will take a look and compare the 18 years prior to the new millennium and 18 years since the new millennium. So from 1982 to 2000, compared to 2000 to 2018.

In terms of returns, if you were to just buy and hold from the beginning of 1982 to the beginning of 2000, the 18 years prior to 2000, the total return of the S&P 500 was approximately 1,100%. From the beginning of 2000 to the beginning of 2018, the last 18 years, the total return of the S&P 500 was approximately 92%. A 1,110% return compared to a 92% return. That's a difference of almost 12 times.

In terms of declines and recovery, between 1982 and 2000, the two biggest drops were Black Monday of 1987, which saw an approximately 36% drop from top to bottom, which took 8 months to break even, and August of 1998 which saw an approximately 23% drop from top to bottom, which took less than 2 months to break even.

In terms of declines and recovery, between 2000 and 2018, the two biggest drops were an approximately 50% drop during the years from early 2000 to early 2003. If you happened to have bought at the peak, it would have taken you about 7.5 years to break even. Then an approximately 57% drop from mid 2007 to early 2009. If you happened to have bought at the peak, it would have taken you about 6 years to break even.

From 1982 to 2000, there was a 23% to 36% drop, with a recovery time of 2 to 8 months, compared to the years from 2000 to 2018, in which there was a 50% to 57% drop, with a recovery time of 6 to 7.5 years. From declines to recoveries, there was a dramatic difference in magnitude.

To summarize, it is important that we recognize and acknowledge that the investment landscape has changed a lot in the last 20 years because many investment strategies and ideologies we still hear today were developed during that comparatively stable and less volatile time. However, due to the changes we have seen in the last 20 years, many of these strategies and ideologies have lost their effectiveness, value, and relevance. The conclusion is, since our investment landscape has changed and evolved, we too need to evolve and adapt our investment strategies to the present. We cannot just keep on blindly using what has worked in the past.

WE INVEST IN OUR BELIEFS, NOT THE MARKETS

As we started off by mentioning, beliefs are very important when it comes to investing. They affect how we invest: if we take charge of our investments ourselves, have someone else invest for us or if we even invest at all. More importantly, I have to stress the importance of adopting the right and proper beliefs because ultimately when we are investing, we are investing in our beliefs. People often think they are investing in the markets, but actually what they are investing in is their beliefs about the markets. This is a critical concept to keep in mind. Personally, understanding and realizing that concept helped take my investments to the next level.

This reality might be a little difficult to wrap our heads around at first, but consider this, the markets behave the same for everyone. If we are just investing in the markets, we should all get similar if not identical results. But we don't. How come some people make more money than others in a rising market, for example? Or how come some are able to profit from a recession while others lose a fortune? The market's behaviour and performance does not vary from one person to another. It is the beliefs about the markets that vary from one person to another. Therefore, one of the main keys to being able to invest successfully is to have the proper beliefs in regards to investing and the markets.

GENUINE INVESTMENT ADVICE AND POOR INVESTMENT ADVICE

Many of our beliefs regarding investments have been acquired and shaped by various pieces of investment advice we've come across over time. And there's all sorts of investment concepts, strategies, and theories. Which ones serves us? Which ones do not? There was a time when it was tough getting information, let alone getting information in a timely manner. But today, with the evolution of technology via computers, smartphones and the internet, we live in a time of information overload. Investment ideas and strategies are a dime a dozen. Almost everyone seems to have an idea of what to do. We come across so many investment ideas and so much advice. Often, the more we learn the more confused we get, as many of these investment ideas seem to contradict each other. How do we organize and conceptualize them all in a context that makes sense? As an individual investor I, too, had to struggle with that problem.

After years of study, research and practical hands-on experience investing my own money, as well as working in the finance and investment sales industry, I was finally able to sort and put everything in context. This belief system is a mental construct meant to organize all the ideas, advice, theories, strategies, and concepts I've accumulated as they relate to investments. I'll just refer to all of that as "investment advice" for simplicity.

It's obvious there's some investment advice that works and some that does not. So, I separate them into two categories: "Genuine Investment Advice" and "Poor Investment Advice." Within those two categories, there are actually two sub-categories we could further separate the investment advice into.

Within Genuine Investment Advice, the first subcategory is investment advice that I believe is almost universal and works for almost everyone. For example, diversification, cutting losses short, letting winners grow, and waiting for favourable risk to return opportunities before investing.

The second subcategory, as well as all the other categories we'll touch upon, is where things get interesting. It's where it causes lots of confusion among people's belief systems and is a source of frustration for many. Within this second sub-category of Genuine Investment Advice is the investment advice that is accurate and works but may not work for everyone, because it depends on their personality and their investment style. For example, many investment ideas, theories, and strategies seem like complete opposites when you compare them with one another: value investing versus momentum investing, swing trading versus momentum investing, fundamental analysis versus technical analysis, short-term trading versus long-term investing, buy low and sell high versus buy high and sell higher, and top down versus bottom up investment styles. All these investment ideas and strategies work, but success depends on how they match the individual investor's personality and how they are used alongside their investment style. In a nutshell, those are examples of Genuine Investment Advice.

On the other end of the spectrum from Genuine Investment Advice we have Poor Investment Advice. It's basically advice that is not effective or does not work. Within this main category, it also has two sub-categories.

In the first sub-category is investment advice that used to work but is outdated because of the change in the investment landscape that we touched upon earlier. It used to work and perhaps even used to deliver great results but has since greatly lost value and effectiveness. Yet, these investment ideas still get passed around by many people because they have failed to recognize that the investment landscape has dramatically changed and evolved in recent years.

Some examples are: index investing, buying and holding indiscriminately, dollar cost averaging, and investing on a consistent and regular schedule regardless of overall market conditions. It's easy to see where such investment ideas, strategies and advice come from once we understand how the investment landscape used to be and what had happened in the past. Like we've seen in our example, the stock market, namely the S&P500, went up approximately 1,100% from 1982 to the year 2000. Yet, in our recent investment landscape from 2000 to the beginning of 2018, the total return of the S&P500 was a mere 92%—a return that's dramatically less than 1/12th in the same 18-year time span. That is less than 10% of the 1,100% return the we've seen from 1982 to the year 2000.

The second subcategory of Poor Investment Advice is the one which I despise the most. They are essentially "investment advice" that was never effective and never worked. For example, advice such as "If you don't sell your losing position, you aren't really losing money because unless you cash out, it's only a paper loss." That is as foolish as saying "If you go to the casino and convert your cash into casino chips, then you lose your chips, you're not actually losing money unless you convert those chips back into cash." Then there's "Adding to losses and losing positions is beneficial because when you average down, it gives you better value and a lower overall price point." With this strategy, you are not only not cutting your losses, you are adding to an already losing position. Technically, you could use this flawed logic to invest in a company as it goes all the way down to bankruptcy because it suggests the lower the price goes, the more you should invest. There is also "Focus on the long-term, and don't worry that your stocks are down because you're still getting paid dividends." Focusing solely on dividends presents a very distorted and partial picture, as you should be focusing on total return which consists of dividends plus any capital gains or losses. With that in mind, if your stock is down -40%, it would be foolish to say it's alright because you're receiving a 3% dividend yield.

People often ask, "If such investment advice doesn't work, then why do people say these things?" The answer is because these ideas mainly originate and get spread around by unscrupulous individuals in the financial and investment industry. In reality, such investment advice was merely conjured up to promote and sell investment products to customers and keep their customers invested so they could continue to charge them various fees and commissions.

Unfortunately, because much of this investment advice came from individuals within the financial and investment industry, it gave them a false sense of credibility and such bad advice got perpetually circulated. This is especially true because the advice is usually mixed in with some rationalization and half truths. When I say half truths, I am also referring to the dated investment advice that we mentioned earlier. I consider those half truths, because those strategies used to work, but have greatly lost significance since. Nevertheless, such bad advice is still often used as sales pitches by individuals in the industry to promote and sell various investment products.

Notice that all such advice falls under a similar underlying idea. It is to tell the customer that it is always a good time to invest and once they are invested, to never sell. For example, when the markets are high, they will say you should invest more because things are going well and you are making money. When the markets are low, they will say you should invest more because you are getting good value. Also, it is always a good time to invest, regardless of how the overall market condition is, because it is supposedly about your time in the markets, not timing the markets. Basically, the message is always geared at giving them your money, keeping it with them and never taking it away, so they can continuously charge you various fees. At the end of the day, if the client makes money, all the better, but even if they don't, the individual and company still gets to charge their fees.

In providing Genuine Investment Advice verses Poor Investment Advice, an individual's salary and bonus often comes in between the two. I'm reminded of a quote from Upton Sinclair: "It is difficult to get a man to understand something, when his salary depends on his not understanding it." However, to be fair, many of those who work in the financial and investment industry are not unscrupulous or ill-intentioned. Like many everyday people, they too, are caught up in the confusion. They come across poor investment advice that they actually believe to be true, which they use themselves and also end up passing on.

ADDITIONAL INVESTMENT TIPS FOR THE EVERYDAY INVESTOR

Make Use of Technical Analysis

As individual investors, we have limited time and resources. I believe the most efficient and effective way for an individual investor to conduct market research and to look for investment opportunities is through the use of technical analysis. Before you get intimidated, technical analysis is basically a fancy way of saying to look at price charts and graphs. You are literally looking at a picture, the big picture. It's efficient because, for example, if I wanted to, I could literally look through hundreds of companies and their price charts in a day. Comparatively, I cannot read through hundreds of annual reports or articles a day.

Keep an Investing Journal

Experiencing losses due to bad judgements or mistakes is part of every investor's journey. Unfortunately, when it comes to investing, making mistakes usually translates to losing money. At least when losses and mistakes occur, try to profit from them by keeping a journal of what happened and how, in an effort to learn from the experience and to not to let it happen again. As the saying goes, "Fool me once, shame on you. Fool me twice, shame on me."

Be Sure to Diversify

Diversification is a simple risk management technique we should all make use of to protect ourselves from the unknown and to improve our risk to return ratio. The simple reason being we can never foresee and predict everything in the markets. During my years of investing, I've seen an oil company whose oil rig was destroyed by a natural disaster; a factory that, due to some employee's negligence, was burned down to a crisp; the CEO of a company who got caught up in various alleged scandals leading to the collapse of the company and, one of my favorites, which is when Tesla's stock price took a sudden dive one day because Elon Musk decided to announce that the company was going bankrupt as an April Fool's Day joke in 2018. No matter how much in-depth research we conduct, nobody could have foreseen any of those events happening. So protect your investment portfolio by diversifying.

Look Beyond "Glam Stocks"

When individuals share their investment holdings with me, I often notice that they have many of the same stock holdings. The reason is they often have what I call "Glam Stocks." These are the glamorous stocks we often hear about in the news and media, the ones our friends and family talk about at dinner parties and gatherings. There is nothing wrong with having those holdings per se, but expand your scope, look further and dig deeper. You will realize that there are plenty of more diverse opportunities out there, many of which are either less volatile and less risky, have more growth potential, have a better performance record or sometimes all of the above. So keep looking and don't settle just for what you hear or see around you.

Know When to Get Out, Before You Get In

Before you get into an investment position, decide when you would exit if things do not go as intended. You are more clear minded before you start an investment. So decide when you would exit if things do not go your way ahead of time, as you will lose objectivity afterwards.

Gradually Ease In and Out of Investments

When investing, especially in stocks, a common practice is to use one entry and one exit into an investment position. Instead of using an all-in or all-out approach, a more strategic risk management approach would be to gradually ease yourself in and out of an investment depending on its subsequent performance. For example, instead of investing $5,000 all at once, consider investing initially only $2,500, then decide if you still want to invest the remaining $2,500 depending on the subsequent performance of the particular investment. Doing this would automatically cut your initial risk by 50%. The same idea applies to getting out of an investment.

Cut Losses and Keep Them Small

When investing, keeping control of our losses is a vital component of risk management. If there is one common piece of advice I've gathered from many great investors, it is that they all cut their losses and keep them small. Considering that most big losses usually started off as small losses, there is no point in letting a small loss grow into a big loss. If you are uncertain about an investment holding, instead of holding all of it or none of it, consider selling a portion of it. For example, if you sell half of it, you will reduce your risk by 50%. Another common culprit that leads investors to hold onto losses is focusing on break-even points and prices. In reality, nobody actually cares where or at what price you bought an investment and where you would break-even. It has no special meaning to anybody other than you and the tax department, so do not focus on that.

Avoid Adding to Losing Positions

When you have a losing investment position, often people believe that buying more will get you better value as you average down your overall price point. That is actually a poor strategy because having a losing position usually means that something you anticipated did not materialize and instead the opposite outcome occurred. There must have been something that was misjudged, overlooked, or unforeseen. Therefore, it does not make strategic sense to add more to an investment which you have already misunderstood and misjudged. Moreover, not only does that go against the concept of keeping your losses small, it is in fact the opposite, because you are adding more money to a losing position.

Remember that You Are Investing in Your Beliefs, Not the Markets

If there is one piece of advice that is more important than controlling your losses, it would definitely be that nobody cares more about your financial well-being than you. So understanding finance and investments is a life skill you should not only acquire but develop, and it all starts with your beliefs. At the core of it all, it is about working on developing your investment belief system.

This requires realigning and readjusting your beliefs and perhaps adopting new ones that serve you, while discarding those that do not. Remember that at the end of the day, we are all just investing in our beliefs.

FINAL THOUGHTS

Finance and investments are one of my greatest passions. I hope I was able to share some fresh perspectives and unique insights on subjects that I personally find to be rarely touched upon or discussed. The ideas and concepts are not exhaustive or complete, however, these are the big ideas, essential concepts and quintessential core beliefs that I've acquired through the years and which really helped propel my investment understanding and financial success.

Often there is nothing worse than to listen to someone advising you on how to reach your goals, when they have not actually reached it themselves. If there was a way for me to turn back time and have the opportunity to sit down with some successful investors who were willing to give me a few important pointers about finance and investing over a cup of coffee or a meal, I hope they would have shared with me the same pointers and beliefs I have shared with you in the last few pages. I know the insights would have definitely made my investment and financial experience a lot smoother and would have helped me reach my financial goals a lot sooner. These beliefs I'm talking about have helped me through many hurdles, make many investment breakthroughs and achieve financial success. I hope they will do the same for you. Remember, "It's Possible!"

For more investment insight, techniques and strategies, visit:

InvestingItWisely.com

Nobody Got Time For That!

The Ultimate Guide For Smart Money Management

URSULA GARRETT

Save, save, save! That's all you hear from family, friends and the media. You are strongly encouraged to save, but how are you supposed to save with a low-paying job, high student loan debt, and the rising cost of housing? Something has got to give – and it's usually not you giving to your savings account. Who has time to be broke when you are young and just want to have fun and enjoy your life? I'll tell you who – nobody. Nobody has got time for that, especially you!

Finances absolutely play a huge part in your life choices and opportunities. Money issues consume chunks of your brain power every day. Think of how many times money (or a lack of it) factors into your decisions throughout your fast-paced day. For instance, you schedule a date on Tinder, buy movie tickets on Fandango and make dinner reservation using Open Table, and you haven't even gotten out of bed yet to start your day. You can do this if you have money in your bank account or power (available credit) on your credit card. Yes, either method of payment will get you what you want right now – one is a smart choice and the other, not so much. You must make smart choices regularly, there is no getting around it.

Size does matter, especially when it refers to your bank account. I want you to recognize that money underwrites the type of life you live and the lack of it means you're not living the life you want to be living. You are forced to make hard choices about what you can afford or what you have to give up. Having limited options make you feel as if your life is less than it could be. Smart money management is the key to your financial goals and personal goals aligning.

Once you recognize that the choices you make with your finances are either limiting your options or providing you opportunities, you can start being more proactive with your finances. First, it is important for you to understand how easy it is to handle your personal business, so you can create real changes that will significantly impact your life.

Two of my five daughters are about the same age, 26 (not twins just a blended family). Throughout their lives, they have taken different paths and made different choices. They are in their mid-twenties now and both spend more than they should, however, one is contributing to a retirement plan and has money go directly from her paycheck into a savings account. The other one lives paycheck to paycheck, has no retirement savings, no personal savings, and is regularly subsidized by her parents. Three guesses which one has more opportunities to live the life she wants, and the first two guesses don't count. While they each had similar opportunities, their individual choices have dictated their current circumstances.

"I am not a product of my circumstances. I am a product of my decisions."

- Stephen Covey

It's a bit of a mystery why you make some of the decisions you make and that's especially true when it comes to your finances. I can tell you from experience that a crystal ball, mesmerizing though it may be, is not where you will find those answers. How often have you made poor financial choices in the moment, only to later regret them and wonder how you got into this situation again? Well, I'm here to tell you that it doesn't matter how or why, what matters is what you do to fix it and make sure it never happens again.

If you have ever paid attention to political elections, then you know how easily you can be fooled by your assumptions, fears and false intuitions. I say this to help you understand that listening to others' opinions about what you should do won't help you reach your goals. Making a plan and following through will.

Which is why I find it useful to understand some principle concepts when you make decisions about money. This is besides, of course, the regular practices of following a budget, saving, investing and avoiding most kinds of debt, factors that I will discuss as part of the steps for smart money management.

These four concepts are the foundation you need for your decision-making process when you are creating your budget or making the decisions about those investments and savings plans. They need to factor into all your financial decisions, because they will help keep you from sabotaging your financial stability.

1) OPPORTUNITY COSTS

No matter what you do or the opportunities that you pursue, there is always going to be a cost. You have to give something to get something. Nothing in life is free. Individually, we get to decide what we are willing to give in exchange. In some circumstances, the price is simply too high, or the payoff is too low to make the deal or take the chance. That threshold is different for everyone and is based on your values.

For example, deciding whether or not to pursue higher education is a decision you make based on your priorities, which could include your financials, your time, and your perception of the value of higher education. Pursuing an advanced degree may take years -- are you willing to put in that amount of time? It could involve giving up other opportunities to finish your degree, but at the same time, the network you build could allow you access to individuals who can create even greater career opportunities in the future. Many individuals choose their university based on the alumni and the type of network they can access for mentors.

Additionally, there is the debt that often comes with pursuing higher education. Are you willing to put yourself into that kind of debt, the type of debt that will take years to pay off? Many individuals see their degree as a doorway to career advancement in a specific field or as a way to pursue the type of work that they are passionate about. For them, the cost of the degree in terms of finances and time is worth it, because they see that degree as an investment in their long-term financial future.

Those two daughters I mentioned earlier, one went to college and has a degree in business and some student loan debt. The other worked part-time jobs and traveled to visit friends she met on the internet. One daughter wanted a college degree and was willing to sacrifice four years of her life, accumulate debt (she considered it as an investment) and forego immediate travel opportunities. The other daughter thought that price was too high. This isn't a matter of right or wrong but a matter of what you are willing to give to get what you want. Here is a general rule of thumb: The bigger the opportunity, the greater the cost or sacrifice to achieve it.

Every decision that you make has all those considerations and it is up to you to give them all a voice before you make your decision. At the same time, your priorities need to guide those smaller financial decisions that we all make throughout the day. Many of your long-term goals are going to be impacted by your short-term decisions. Therefore, giving yourself guidelines for daily spending based on your priorities will help you to reach those goals. Still, not everything can be quantified in terms of your return on investment, as I will explore next.

2) SUNK COSTS

What is sunk cost? This is money you can't get back -- a non-refundable airline ticket, for example. There are certain expenses that you will have throughout your life that are not going to bring a tangible return on investment. In fact, they are likely going to result in nothing more than an enjoyable experience or a pleasant memory. It can be easy to get into a mindset that has you spending far beyond what you may have budgeted or prioritized because you value the experience, but it can put you in a financial bind later. The idea here is that you need to keep sunk costs in proper perspective. It's easy to start thinking, "Well, I've already spent $100, so what's another $25?" My mother always told me not to throw good money after bad. She taught me to understand the concept of sunk costs long before I took a business class. You have got to be willing to walk away sometimes and keep the money in your pocket for other investment opportunities.

Once something is paid for, and cannot be refunded, it shouldn't impact your future financial decisions. It is a "sunk" cost, i.e. water under the bridge, and no matter what you do in the future you won't ever get it back. Therefore, you can't allow yourself to get hung up on the moments where you spent money in a way that didn't fall into your overall financial plan. In the end, you have to accept that sunk costs are going to happen and make your peace with them. Recognize that you will buy emotionally and defend rationally, even if that might not always be wise. There are costs that are simply not recoupable.

Regrets over sunk costs can make it harder to move forward, leaving you vulnerable to make other choices that you may not have otherwise made. Do not allow yourself to fall into the downward spiral. Negative thoughts often breed more negative thoughts, especially if you continue to dwell on them. The same can be said for financial decisions. When you focus on your bad financial decisions, you may find yourself repeating them, because that is your focus.

It is important to keep yourself focused on ways to improve your financial decisions and keep them in line with your financial plan. Yes, you might regret a decision, but make the conscious choice not to dwell on it. Instead, learn from it and move forward. Life, especially when it comes to finances, is a series of learning experiences. The better you are at accepting the lessons, the better decisions you will be able to make in the future. I find inspiration and humor in the lyrics of one of my favorite songs by Chumbawamba, "I get knocked down, but I get up again, you're never gonna keep me down."

Now that you have that mindset (and that song stuck in your head), you can keep yourself from making financial decisions based on your sunk costs and focus on maximizing your earnings. That starts by focusing on finding the right investments for you. With that in mind, let's talk about the Rule of 72.

3) QUICK INTEREST CALCULATIONS USING THE RULE OF 72

One of your biggest concerns about an investment should be, "What am I going to get out of this?" While you wouldn't want to ask that of a date, it's perfectly acceptable, in fact it's expected, to ask that of a potential investment. All of us want a way to determine the upside of a financial opportunity. Now there are several ways to analyze a financial investment, but it often comes down to how long it will take for an investment to pay off. Want to double your holdings? The Rule of 72 can tell you how long it will take, based on the specific interest rate. Just divide 72 by the interest rate to learn how long it will take to double your initial investment.

For example, if you are looking at an investment with an interest rate of 6 percent, then 72 divided by 6 gets you 12 years. You can then take that information and use it to determine if that timeframe will work with your overall financial plan. Granted, you may find that other factors will play a part in determining your return as well, but it is important to have an idea of what you can expect before you put money into an investment.

This is a rough estimate, of course, but it's pretty effective. Recognize that you might find that a return is going to take significantly longer to make you money. So even if you find it an interesting opportunity, you may opt to not invest in order to take advantage of a different opportunity that will give you a faster return on your money.

In fact, you can also turn the equation around to determine the interest rate you are looking at if someone promises to double your returns in a set amount of time. Twice as much money in 12 years? Divide 72 by 12 and you get an interest rate of 6 percent. This rule lets you evaluate investment opportunities quickly and decide where to put your money in a way that will help you to grow your investments to meet long-term financial goals.

Keep in mind, future earnings are not something that you can count on, so how you use the dollars that you have now are going to have greater weight than potential earnings. You know that old saying, "Don't count your chickens before the eggs hatch."

4) THE TIME VALUE OF MONEY

According to this concept, a dollar you receive today is worth more than a dollar you will get tomorrow. You will have opportunity to invest that dollar immediately and begin earning more revenue from it (and also avoid losing value because of inflation).

It is important to recognize that money from your investments needs to be put to work. Don't be quick to spend it. Making frivolous or useless purchases means you are making a choice to spend on meaningless things and activities and in doing so, you are draining your ability to invest and grow. Focus on how you can essentially create a chain of investments, all working to grow an income stream for you to use in retirement or even for a big purchase that is part of your financial plan (think a house or car). Growth is a long-term process and it is imperative that you do make the time for it.

When you are waiting for an investment to pay off, then you are waiting for your money to work for you. One of the ways that you can save money is by limiting your interest payments. When you are making money from investments, which is then reinvested, you create an income stream that can allow you to pay cash for items, or put down a larger down payment, thus helping to reduce those interest payments, or eliminate them altogether.

Again, this helps you make certain calls about your purchases -- and your income. It's the old "one bird in the hand is worth two in a bush" theory in action for your wallet.

These four concepts have served me well over the years. Now let's focus in on the five steps that will help you to remain financially sound as you invest and grow your income to meet your financial goals.

WHY MONEY MATTERS

Before I talk about the steps, I want you to understand that money has a place and purpose in your life. Whatever adventures or experiences you want to have, you are going to need money to do it. That money is also going to be a key part of fulfilling your life's purpose, simply because money is a resource that can help you get things done. Regardless of if your goal in life is to have a non-profit that helps others or to create a company to bring a product or process to market, the truth is that money will be a resource that you need.

Since you and I can agree on that, let's start talking about your financial goals by first talking about your life goals.

STEP 1 - BUDGETING: YOUR PERSONAL BUSINESS PLAN

You have goals you want to accomplish, experience, and create in this life. This is simply a reality we all share. By defining your goals, you are able to determine what financial moves are necessary to achieve them. Too often, personal goals are overlooked or under-appreciated when creating a financial plan. Your personal goals and your financial plan need to be in sync for you to be successful at achieving either one.

For instance, if you know that your financial plan is going to allow you to achieve your personal goals, then it will help you maintain the excitement and vision you have for your life. This knowledge will help keep up the momentum during tough times or difficult circumstances when you are making sacrifices.

Budgeting should be the first part of your financial plan, because it will show the money you have coming in and going out. Once you understand your cash flow, then you have all the information you need to make a sound financial plan. Your budget will allow you to make good choices about how you want to use your money and where you can make changes in your spending habits to align your personal goals with your financial goals.

As part of that budgeting process, you need to look at the choices you make on a daily basis. Consider that if you take out that Tinder date on Saturday night maybe you can't afford to play golf on Sunday. If you really want to golf, then maybe you have to Netflix and chill with $1 bottles of beer or a $7 bottle of wine and takeout pizza instead of your dinner and a movie date. We all have to make choices. Just make sure your choices are good choices. You may find that you are sabotaging yourself by the financial decisions you make every day.

The good news is that you don't have to try to figure out a budget on your own or hire a professional to do it for you. All you need is that device that sometimes acts as another appendage – your cell phone. Yes, there is another reason that your cell phone is your best friend because there's an app for that (for budgeting, that is). Actually, there are several apps for that, you just have to choose the one that works best for you.

I use Mint to track my personal bank accounts, credit cards, investments and bills – it creates a budget based on my income and expenses and reminds me when I have a payment due date. I love that my whole financial life is accessible in one place and that I can monitor activity at a glance. One of my daughters uses Clarity Money, which has similar features plus the added benefit of helping to cancel unwanted subscriptions. With an app, you won't have to wonder if you are spending too much money shopping or eating out, you can see it in full color. Knowledge is power, and this knowledge can be used to change your spending behavior to match your financial goals.

For instance, think about that $5 cup of coffee you stop to buy every morning to start your day. That money falls into the sunk costs pot, because you are not getting that money back and it is not working for you. Imagine how much money you could save if you took that $5 per day for a year and saved or invested it – you would have more than $1,825. Going back to those two daughters of mine, one likes to buy and play internet games, a lot – can you guess which one? I'll tell you it's not the one that uses Clarity Money. If you are having trouble saving to meet your long-term goals, then it might be worth exploring using an app to help you get control of your spending.

It is not about giving up your lifestyle, but making your lifestyle adhere to your financial priorities, instead of letting your lifestyle dictate your priorities. Everyone has time to know their money.

Part of achieving any financial goal is to create a nest egg of funds to work with, which serves as a basis for your investment portfolio. Using your budget, you can designate a specific percentage to go into your savings.

STEP 2 – SAVING

The point of saving is to create a financial resource that you can use to build your income streams. These income streams can be diversified, but the point is that saving has to be a priority in order to improve your financial situation and allow you to reach your goals. Here are just a few reasons why saving is important.

1. You have a nest egg for emergencies. Time and time again, financial emergencies have sunk individuals who appear to be doing well, simply because they had nothing to fall back on. Once it happens, they have a financial issue, one that can have a ripple effect across other areas of their lives. Point blank, having an emergency, such as an unexpected car repair or house repair, should not financially sink you. Experts recommend that your savings for emergency needs to cover six months of your living expenses. Once you reach that goal, keep saving a set amount to grow your emergency fund. If you have to use some of it for an emergency, then replace it as soon as possible.

2. You can save for larger purchases. You know that paying cash for items can save you money in the long run, because you won't pay interest on top of the purchase cost. When you designate savings for specific

purchases, it allows you to reach your financial goals without acquiring payments. Plus, once you make that big purchase, you can start saving for the next big item or event.

3. You can save to invest to build income streams. Once you have achieved your emergency savings goal, start building a savings that is specifically for investments. These funds should not be used for any other purpose, allowing you to adjust the rate of return to meet your goals.

Clearly, saving is important because it gives you a stepping stone to meet your financial needs and personal dreams. Now, I want to transition to the exploring the possibilities that you can create with a savings that was started for investing.

STEP 3 – INVESTING

When you reach the point that you have started an investment savings account, you have plenty of opportunities. From stocks and bonds to direct investing in a business, you have multiple ways to grow your investment dollars. That being said, it is important to choose investments that fall in line with your goals and your risk tolerance level.

For instance, if you are at the beginning of your career, you might find yourself more inclined to look for high return, risky investments. Why? Many of those who are younger see time on their side and recognize that they have time to recover from a loss. Alternately, as you reach specific benchmarks or get closer to achieving your financial goals, you will start to make less risky investments.

Another potential scenario is that you are planning to get married or start a family, in which case, you might be more concerned with the risk of losing the primary financial provider. In a case like this, you may be more interested in investing in a disability or life insurance policy or even starting a college fund. After all, not all investments are created equal.

Where you are in your life can play a large part in what type of investments you choose to take on. Additionally, you might take on investments that are less time-consuming because they give you the ability to do more of what you enjoy. On the other hand, you might want to be more hands-on in your investments, so that may be a factor in the types of investments you choose.

Your investment plan should be personalized to you and designed to meet your needs. I want you to recognize that working with a financial advisor can help you to determine the best investments for you.

Many of the individuals I work with even consider investing in themselves, which means starting their own business. If you want to explore your entrepreneurial spirit, that can be a great way to invest and see your returns grow, using your investment dollars and sweat equity. Again, I encourage you to put any investment up against your financial plan. Ask yourself the hard questions about whether it will work towards accomplishing your goals. Doing so is critical to keeping you focused and on the path to achieving both your financial and personal goals. Just keep in mind that it takes time to grow and any time frames set by you can be changed, especially if the situation changes.

STEP 4 – AVOIDING MOST KINDS OF DEBT

Debt can drown you financially and make it difficult for you to achieve your financial goals. When you look at your budget, do you see areas where you are spending money on payments regularly? That is money which is not being used to create income streams or to reach your financial goals.

Be picky when you are choosing to take on debt. I recommend that you only finance things that will bring in money or pay for themselves. It's okay to finance your education because you expect your education to yield you a higher paying career. Do not finance your vacation because you will have nothing but memories to show for it. You can pay for your business advertising with a credit card but not your groceries. Avoid running up your credit cards, leaving yourself strapped with payments. The interest payments can quickly exceed your budget and be a drain. Use the cash in your bank account to pay for your living expenses because the interest on credit cards is usually greater than the interest you earn on money deposited in the bank.

Some debt can be beneficial and preferable because it shares the risk. I am talking about debt that involves investing. For instance, if you are building a real estate portfolio of rentals and you have $100,000 to invest, you might find that you choose to split that $100,000 into down payments for five properties instead of just buying one for $100,000. The reason is that you can increase your cash flow across five properties and they can also cover their own overhead. In the meantime, you are creating equity that you can tap into later to purchase more properties. The point is that you want to use your investment cash to maximize your income opportunities. Do not limit yourself because you want to avoid all debt – some debt can be good.

When weighing your debt options, be sure to look at interest rates. Do not feel as if you are limited to one lender or one financing option. Shop around and make sure that you get the lowest possible rate for your debt with the best payment plan to meet your investment needs. Also, make sure that any investment purchased with debt is going to have a positive cash flow. Some investments may not have a positive cash flow initially but will overtime as the debt is paid down. For other investments, it is the value which grows over time that offsets the lack of a positive cash flow.

Again, it is important to work with a professional who can help you determine what types of debt you want to take on regarding your investments and what debt you want to avoid.

In the end, this step is mostly focused on helping you to avoid debt that drains you financially, without giving you any type of return. Think about the cost of those daily coffees. The focus of this step needs to be on defining the lifestyle you want and then investing in order to be able to afford it. If you opt to live a lifestyle that drains your investments, you could be shortchanging yourself for the future, thus limiting your ability to reach your dreams.

STEP 5 – EVALUATE AND ASSESS: ONGOING PROCESS

I call this step, "the shit happens" part of your plan. Yes, it would be nice if life happened exactly as we planned it, but real life is no fairy tale. The reality is that you made a plan based on the life you wanted to live and all the messy stuff that got in your way is why you had contingency plans, emergency funds and cushions built into your plan. Shit happens, and you deal. You deal by adapting to your new situation. Update your plan as if it is a living, breathing organism.

For instance, you had an accident that kept you from working for six months. That would be both physically and financially draining. This is only a temporary setback. Now you need to reset your goals to achieve your plans, because you may need to focus on rebuilding instead of growth. Still, the point is to make adjustments that help you achieve your goals, thus not allowing the circumstances to overwhelm you and derail your finances permanently.

This need to make adjustments also applies to your investments. I recommend at least once per quarter that you review your investments to make sure they are performing as expected. You don't want to waste your resources on underperforming investments.

Are there areas you might want to expand even further, or do you need to eliminate some investments because they no longer fit your financial goals? Doing these reviews regularly can help you to keep your financial life on track with your personal life. When the two are in sync, then you will find that your life continues to improve. This harmony makes it possible to achieve what you want, no matter the setbacks you might occasionally encounter.

Keep in mind that evaluating and assessing will always be ongoing processes. The fluidity of life is that you can create plans, but events may alter those plans or even offer you new opportunities and experiences that you might not have even considered.

It is important to keep your mind open, both to new investments and to new experiences and opportunities in your personal life. They often can dovetail together more than you ever realize.

Financially, your world is built on the decisions that you make throughout your life. Always know the direction you want to go before you start your journey. When you make decisions without direction, your life will be like a boat without a rudder. It goes all over but doesn't actually get anywhere. The waves take the boat in multiple directions without a clear destination.

I want you to define your path and then work in harmony with that by making choices to complement it. Even with a defined path, it can be easy to make decisions that run contrary to your goals, as I discussed earlier in this chapter. When I work with individuals, I help them to not only define their path, but also to determine the types of goals that align with their paths. Then, I can help them to find the right investments and set financial goals to help them go further on that path.

Growth happens by learning from those people who inspire you to do and be more. We all have time to learn and grow.

Please email Ursula Garrett at ugarrett@cpagarrett.com or visit her website www.cpagarrett.com

Project Management

How to be Extremely Efficient and Remain Profitable While Developing Any Project

GUSTAVO A. VALENZUELA

The Project Management Institute (PMI) officially defines project management as the application of knowledge, skills, tools and techniques to project activities to meet the project requirements.

To properly manage any project, you must have acquired, through actual management experience, specific knowledge pertinent to the needs of the project. Furthermore, as a project manager, you must have skills in negotiation, decision making, trust building, crisis management, conflict management and verbal and oral communication. These skills and more are needed to remain in control of the entire project's team and their performance. However, being able to visualize and fully understand the project as a whole is probably the best ability you can have and is necessary in order to know immediately, at any phase and at any given time, if the project is moving forward in the best possible way.

LOPPM (LACK OF PROPER PROJECT MANAGEMENT)

In many situations, project owners without a project manager can only appreciate the services of a seasoned project manager when the project is in crisis and they are desperately seeking help. This is not an unusual situation, as people will often take on projects without fully understanding what they are getting into. They'll sign the contract, then get slammed by the intricacies of the project. and the many requirements and processes they must follow, without realizing that an experienced project manager is the ideal person capable of delivering the project within scope, schedule and budget.

While working closely with project owners, I concentrate on increasing their involvement in the entire project development. As a result, they're thrilled to feel in control of their project, especially their budget. They truly appreciate having my experience and expert advice as I act as their project manager. If you would like to benefit from the services of an experienced project manager, please visit www.TheBookonPM.com

WHO RUNS PROJECT MANAGEMENT?

You, as the hired project manager, are responsible for running all such entities, while also keeping in mind that stakeholders may influence your process, something that deserves to be seen as an opportunity for you to remain in control of managing the project—as long as you hold them accountable and make them aware that budget, project schedule and scope may be affected by their requests and attempts to run your project.

WHAT IS AND WHAT IS NOT PROJECT MANAGEMENT?

Initially, your main goal is to select the most effective and ideal team that will run itself without micro or macro managing every aspect and assigned task. If you're successful and your budget can afford to assemble a team of experts, the project will most likely run smoothly (as long as you're able to properly manage it). Having the best team doesn't mean you can stop acting as the project manager. You must also watch all aspects and processes; the scope, compliance, the budget and the schedule. Allowing things to happen and disconnecting your management eye from a project because you've established trust and confidence in the team's abilities isn't really considered project management.

Even when you have the best team to develop your project, a successful project manager is always looking for opportunities to improve the process, to save money, to be more efficient and perhaps even to discover new ways to improve the bottom line. There are opportunities with every project to adjust, improve and even systemize processes to become more efficient, to stay engaged throughout the entire process and to capitalize on those opportunities. By performing your duties as a project manager at all times, your expertise and level of confidence will be elevated and will rightfully separate you from amateur project managers seeking to complete a project just as required.

When you ask yourself "What is Project Management?" you may now add, "The ability to remain connected and engaged throughout the entire process in order to positively affect scope, budget and schedule."

A ROBUST DEFINITION FOR PROJECT MANAGEMENT

As you work in project management, you'll realize the importance of taking your duty as a project manager beyond your contractual agreement. You are already expected to apply your knowledge, your skills and your techniques to meet the project requirements. But by choice, you must make it a personal practice to consciously look for the greatest benefit for the project regardless of what is in your project manager contract.

Project management is inclusive of moral values for both personnel and stakeholders, project managers must also have proper understanding while managing diverse personalities, cultural differences and beliefs. Your decision to go beyond management of project scope, budget, schedule, risk, quality and resources sets you apart from the herd.

How will you know when you are going the extra mile? When you come to that situation in which you tell yourself "This is outside my contractual duties," but you're certain that if properly addressed and handled it will positively influence the outcome of the project—and you simply choose to do it.

To download guidelines on effective steps and ideas on how you may push yourself to consistently go the extra mile, please visit www.TheBookonPM.com

Last, in a new definition of project management, you could easily add,

"The ability to include everything tied to any project and place it under the responsibility of a qualified project manager who's able to handle whatever arises, always taking action for the benefit of the project." That would be an all-inclusive contract only a few project managers would confidently sign. If you include yourself in that list of the selected few that would sign such a contract, you are a project manager at heart.

WHY PROJECT MANAGEMENT?

Anyone with the financial means to do so can develop an intent to manage a project without the proper knowledge and specific experience. However, the results will not be favorable for any of the variables that matter, such as scope, budget and schedule. The truth is they will lose money—in the millions—as a result of their innocence and obvious unsophistication in the subject. In the United States, around 68% of the projects fail in at least one of the three critical areas and 98% of those failed projects lacked the services of a project manager. Even more revealing, the remaining 32% of the projects that did not fail were properly organized and managed by an experienced workforce and included the services of an experienced project manager. More so, for every billion invested in the United States, $122 million is wasted due to lack of project performance and proper management. Even more shocking, the failure rate is 50% higher for projects with budgets over $1 million. In most cases, the project owner doesn't even know they are losing money or that they are overspending.

Next time you are acting as a project sponsor or if you are the actual project owner, realize that you may not have the correct talent in your organization to properly develop a project. Additionally, make the right choice and wisely avoid assigning your project and its management to an inexperienced workforce.

EFFECTS OF HAVING AN EXPERIENCED PROJECT MANAGER

The simplest way of saying this is that having an experienced project manager in your development team managing every aspect of your project is the equivalent of having a cardiovascular surgeon perform open heart surgery on you rather than the Chief Executive Officer (CEO) of the hospital. Only project managers can do the job of a project manager, despite the common belief that anybody in the team can wear multiple hats and perform several duties. The effects of having an experienced project manager will indeed be favorable and noticeable, always revolving around success.

LOSING CONTROL AND MONEY

The margin for keeping or losing control of your project is very narrow. There are a number of factors that can be directly related to losing control of your project. Scope creep, departing staff, wrong skill sets being allocated to the project ad lack of focus from the project team can all lead to disaster and you losing control of the project.

Managing tasks, keeping an open communication line with your active team members and setting the stage for upcoming team members are all good practices for staying in control. Many outside factors may also cause you to lose control of the project and if that is the case, your immediate attention is required. Take a step back and reassess the situation as a whole. Once you've gained complete understanding and a clear picture, you may develop a plan to begin turning the project around and back on track. As soon as you identify and begin to tackle a challenge, you have begun gaining control of the project.

Losing money in a project is often tied to key pieces of information being excluded or overpriced by vendors and which are crucial for a successful project completion. You must also have a well-developed ability to review and negotiate bids, quotes or any costs associated with the project. Hence, it is vital that a project manager has the project owner first review the entire project scope and then approve all proposed costs for the correct and just amount of money. Project owners tend to ignore these critical initial operations. At the end, this translates to loss of revenue via wasteful unnecessary spending to the point that your project is not fully completed or ready for occupancy.

To download guidelines and a checklist on effective steps you may take to avoid or stop losing control and money, please visit www.TheBookonPM.com

ACCOUNTABILITY OF STAKEHOLDERS

As a project manager, you're required and expected to execute processes and move through project phases in a clear way so that the planning and approving process for scope is definitive and formal, as to avoid and minimize changes. Hence, when any stakeholder—including the project owner or sponsor—requests a change in scope, budget or schedule you can hold them accountable for what they've requested. People, in general, change their minds constantly and if you're one of those project managers who make challenging and impossible projects seem easy because of your expertise, organizational skills and outstanding people skills, owners will feel invited to propose changes anytime they feel like it. There's a lot at stake and it's your duty to communicate and paint a clear picture for all stakeholders. Formally and officially remind the project owner about the process for approval of scope then pull out and present their approval document with their signed name, signature and date. Point out the paragraph addressing "changes in scope" in which, in sum, it communicates that after approval, and especially during the middle of production, any changes in scope will drastically and most definitely affect budget and schedule. If the owner is still adamant about his request, prepare the correct documents and amend the project's budget to properly compensate your team for accommodating such a late request.

HOW MANY PHASES ARE FOUND IN PROJECT MANAGEMENT?

As a project manager you'll go through the basic phases in any of the projects you're managing. These phases may include: initiating, planning, execution/ production, monitoring/controlling and closing or close out phase. These are the general overall main phases or, in simple terms, the summary of the whole picture.

As a project manager, it is advantageous if you choose to see subphases within major phases. A phase is simply a grouped set of goals or requirements containing a number of steps. Once completed in the allocated time, that phase has been attained and the project can progress to the next phase. So, it's for your own benefit, as you become an extraordinary project manager, to identify what those subphases are in your project.

By breaking down a phase into subphases or a major set of goals into individual goals, you have created a daily, weekly or monthly to-do list to execute your job as an effective project manager. Moving from goal to goal or from point A to point B has new meaning. This simple technique will allow you to visualize and understand the whole picture of any project and at the same time, it will allow you to see and understand the smallest detail of the project.

WHEN TO ENGAGE A PROJECT MANAGER

As a project owner or sponsor, as soon as you get an idea to develop a project, call a project manager and hire him to assist and represent you in the entire process. Nonetheless, at any phase of the project a seasoned project manager can keep things clear, honest and legal. A project manager can hold everybody accountable and in strict compliance with their contractual obligations, on behalf of the project owner and in consideration of established goals of the project. The earlier a project manager is engaged, the more beneficial it is for stakeholders and the project variables, including scope, budget and schedule.

To hire and benefit from having the expert advice of a project manager in your organization, please visit www.TheBookonPM.com

EFFICIENCY DEFINITION THROUGH A PROJECT MANAGER'S LENS

Improving your abilities and skills to manage scope, time, quality, costs and risks logically and habitually happens after you completely understand projects as a whole and after having the benefit of actually managing several projects from start to end and beyond

Only when choosing to know all the project details and team requirements is efficiency born. Then you as the project manager acting as a project leader and working closely with stakeholders can define critical project milestones. Having open communication allows you as the project manager to attain pertinent documentation required to easily move the project forward. Equally as important, understanding and managing risks on a daily basis and taking corrective action will drastically improve overall efficiency.

HOW TO GET AN "A-TEAM"

The success of your project is based in great part on the quality of experience of your selected team members. Therefore, during team selection, first seek for relevant, proven and verifiable experience that is as close as possible to the requirements of your project type. Second, look for people with strong abilities to solve problems and verify they have the right knowledge and access to tools to tackle the most complex challenges the project may face. Third, evaluate their longevity and stability in the specific tasks they're working on. Last, ask them to enlist their strengths and explain why they're interested in becoming part of your team. Always check the validity of all information as submitted and do verify their references.

After accomplishing full compliance with the project's legal requirements, you may assist the procurement team with verifying the project's technical and special requirements. Intentionally choose a diverse selection committee with specific expertise in different areas of the development, including scope, execution, finance, policy, technical, maintenance, warranty, life cycle, or other areas identified as important to the specifics of the project.

Once you have performed all these duties, you ought to consider receiving from all vendors a formal statement or summary of qualifications (SOQ) as part of the documenting process. Gather, review and rank all information, and then interview the top five vendors.

To download a smart list of SOQ items, please visit www.TheBookonPM.com

THE RIGHT INTERVIEW QUESTIONS

Efficient project management is directly related to efficient use of time and opportunities. Utilize the interview to ask only questions that will give you a new insight into the vendor's knowledge, expertise or specific skills. Also, use the interview time to ask the tough questions vendors are not usually asked.

When submitting a written SOQ, the vendor has all the time in the world to formulate a written answer. However, during an interview the vendor only has seconds or minutes to formulate and give his response. As a result, his response is real and it informs you how this particular vendor will handle things during the development process. It's easy for a vendor to state in writing that they have years of experience and can handle your project, but during the interview, if you formulate real questions based on actual project requirements, you'll be able to tell if that vendor is truly knowledgeable and has the right procedures and tools to move the project forward.

Ask questions about all critical areas of the process, including, initiation, planning, execution, monitoring and controlling, closing out, warranty, operational phase and sustainability. This line of questioning truly filters vendors. Those with real, honest experience are able and willing to share their answers in great detail. Then, verify their response by calling their references.

To rely on the expert advice of a project manager to guide your team during vendor interviews, please visit www.TheBookonPM.com

EFFICIENT WAYS TO GET YOUR PROJECT DONE

After you wisely organize processes and all project tasks are properly delegated, you must concentrate on maximally producing or realizing tasks on that specific day; Verify that critical tasks' requirements are clearly identified, that the required work for execution has been delegated to the right party. Then verify the project is performed as planned. Always be two steps or more ahead of your own schedule. Before, during and even after project development, continuously ask yourself "How can I be more efficient?" Any and all ideas that come to mind, simply try them out. If they're successful, choose to make them part of your process on all your future projects.

ORGANIZATION BASED ON EFFICIENCY AND FLOW

The number of people and tasks required to properly and successfully complete a complex project is immense. Subsequently, intending to keep track of them all in your mind is not an efficient way to get your project done. A single organizational chart depicting names, assigned tasks (below stakeholder's titles) and properly organized by the project's phases allows for an efficient way to channel information for proper review and approval. Indeed, an entire project's directory is an important document to keep updated for the benefit of effective project management. Relying on a complete organizational chart is a clear way to see the entire picture, including the review and approval process for each of the project phases.

Organizational charts with detailed information regarding the review and approval process can show the flow of important information either up or down. Up information may include items such as change order requests, payment application requests or allowance use authorizations. Down flow information may include an instance when an owner requested a change in scope, a failed inspection report or a corrective action plan. If an owner sees graphically, in an organizational chart, how many people he's affecting with his "simple request to change scope" he or she may reconsider his request.

Use a detailed organizational chart as a tool for stakeholders to realize the importance of understand positioning and flow in the project's team. As a result, this will create continuity and efficiency.

RECOGNIZE THE ACTUAL STATUS OF YOUR PROJECT

As you create your progress summary report, make a commitment to be completely honest as you report on scope, budget, timeline, risks, quality and percentage completed. Sometimes owners get feedback from other sources and honesty will be your best practice if it comes down to verifying the validity of your report. Reporting on all areas of the project helps your efficiency and saves time as you avoid having several separate meetings.

If the project risk is high on any project area, formulate potential solutions on how to mitigate or eliminate such risks. Any solutions you present ideally you've already discussed with your team prior to presenting them to the project owner. It's important to report on key areas without inundating stakeholders with too much information, especially if it is technical information.

Staying in control of the project also allows stakeholders to sense and see that the project is in great hands and that you are on top of things and two steps ahead.

MONOTONY = BORED DISCONNECTED TEAM

It's true that repetition makes you better at anything, however, during project development, a lack of variety and interest paired with a tedious routine may affect the moral and emotional well-being of your team. Anytime you have a team who is bored working on your project, you're close to having a team that is disconnected from your project. After disconnect comes inefficiency and inevitable mistakes or inaccuracy with scope compliance.

There are many ways you can avoid monotony or promote variability. One way is to allow your team members to fully understand the project's mission and not just the task at hand. You may choose to reward an early finish and accuracy as a way to keep the team excited about accelerating their portion of the work and being accurate and in full compliance with scope.

You may also share some exciting news about the project such as plans to submit for a worldwide recognition award or being acknowledged on important social media sites as a way to recognize them for their portion of the work. The main idea is to avoid monotony and make your team feel appreciated. You want to periodically remind them that their portion of the project is just as important and meaningful as the rest.

For other great ideas on how to keep your team motivated, please visit www.TheBookonPM.com and download a complete list of ideas and techniques, which will keep your team energized and connected to your project.

SYSTEMIZING THE PROCESS

Ideally, your system model wisely accommodates individual expression. This means that as long as the team's creative choices during execution yield the established and required system results, team members can decide how and in what ways their execution may be more fun, efficient and varied. The goal of having a system is to create organization and improve predictability. Furthermore, a system allows for new team members to enter the system and become productive in the least amount of time possible.

Having expert skills and knowledge in a particular field drastically increases your accuracy when completing a specialized task. For instance, you may recognize that your expertise in project management is what gives value to your daily work and your brand. Likewise, recognizing your team's individual expertise will allow you to properly delegate tasks and increase accuracy to the point of achieving perfection.

ELEMENTS OF A GREAT SCHEDULE

A schedule is basically WHAT needs to done, by WHEN and WHO is responsible for it. The project schedule is also required to comply with contractual milestones and it must be formulated with the level of detail required by the contract.

Schedules can serve as a daily, weekly and monthly guide and they're a reliable tool to verify estimated versus actual progress for the completed portion of the project. The level of detail or task description in a schedule varies depending on whom the schedule is written for and what the true intent is for having it.

You may also consider adding enough information to allow listed tasks to act like a to-do list. In fact, including critical reviews and approvals and listing an inspector's information may be extremely practical and beneficial. Adding the sequence for review and approval and listing appointed personnel to perform such duties will be a great way to organize and make the entire team aware of critical inspection events.

Note: Every time you catch yourself thinking "I need to remind myself to do this," and that specific task is not on the schedule, simply add it and test if having such information listed is beneficial to the entire team.

LOOK FURTHER INTO CRITICAL TASKS

Is it possible to dig deeper into critical tasks and find information worth sharing on the project schedule? Absolutely! If you further investigate and understand who is at the bottom of any task or performing any type of work, including review or approval, then adding their information to the schedule will provide you with another level of management. Make a practice to identify every single person involved in any of the processes. By doing so, you'll be able to expedite compliance with that specific task.

FACTORS SHAPING YOUR SCHEDULE

There are other factors shaping or affecting a project's schedule and knowing these factors exist helps the team to plan and allocate time just in case they arrive. Although some of these factors impacting your project schedule, such as climate and accidents, are completely outside your control, you may still formulate a plan to mitigate their effects on your schedule. In the case of climate, knowing climate trends and identifying rainy seasons can help you plan for such an event.

Other factors difficult to plan or accommodate in your schedule include sick people, new hires, new trends, changes in scope, additional safety, omissions, new regulations, unforeseen conditions, etc. You, as the project manager working with your team, may formulate and agree on a plan of action to take if any of the previous factors happen to arrive during your project. Having an agreed plan of attack drastically reduces downtime and excuses for not having a potential solution in place.

HOW TO ADDRESS UNFORESEEN CONDITIONS

In every project, unforeseen conditions and events arrive and test your skills and ability to find solutions. There are some basic steps you must take in order to address unforeseen conditions. First, immediately attend to it by identifying who's in charge of that specific portion of the project. Secondly, once you identify the appropriate party, perform an internal "911" or urgent phone call to the individual in charge to explain the emergency and the urgency for them to address the issue at hand immediately. Third, look at your schedule for float and identify items you may borrow time from to address the unforeseen condition. Then take necessary measures to resolve the issue effectively. Last, choose to plan ahead of time for unforeseen conditions by creating an allowance in your budget for such situations. One of the main reasons unforeseen conditions do not get immediately attended is because there are no funds allocated to pay for the required resources to solve the matter at hand.

Follow the steps listed above on every project you manage and you'll certainly handle any unforeseen condition as a true professional in charge of managing the entire project development.

To benefit from the expert advice of a project manager, to receive assistance reviewing your project's documents or to identify potential unforeseen conditions prior to officially starting your project, please visit www.TheBookonPM.com

WHAT CREATES UNWANTED CHALLENGES IN A PROJECT

Unwanted challenges are often created by unrealistic owner expectations with scope, budget or schedule. Also, inadequate project funding and an inexperienced owner or stakeholder making critical project decisions will always result in an undesirable turn of events. It's common to invite unwanted challenges as early as when procuring and selecting a team if selection is solely based on costs instead of experience or expertise. Even as you review and approve their contracts, having insufficient contractual responsibilities will invite your team and project to face unwanted challenges. As a project manager, the inability to exercise stakeholder accountability may also bring unnecessary, challenging situations to the project. Once unwanted challenges arrive, the project may enter into crisis.

THE CRISIS MANAGER

If you're ever invited to handle a project in crisis, it's a clear sign that you've gained the respect and trust from the project owner, a sponsor or your employer. If you're a great, experienced project manager, you probably have gained the respect and trust from all three entities already. Project managers who can see the big picture and understand every phase and every single detail of the complete development of a project can in fact and will certainly jump on the opportunity to take over a project in crisis. It's like a doctor performing surgery on a patient diagnosed as inoperable or incurable. The doctor goes in with all he's got and does what he does best and cures a patient deemed incurable.

Once assigned to handle a project in crisis you must assume the responsibility of solving any and all project issues and challenges without assigning blame. It's the professional and right thing to do. Let attorneys do their job, when their services are engaged. Managing a project in crisis is about finding solutions and implementing the best solutions to gain control of the project and by having a clear mission to get it back on track. Your immediate goal ought to be to do whatever it takes to guide it and manage it to a successful completion.

When you act as a crisis manager it's a perfect opportunity to display your knowledge, expertise and acquired specialized management abilities. If, on the other hand, you're a project owner or a sponsor, keep in mind that one sure way to get your entire team and your project into a crisis is to choose to develop a project without the services of an experienced project manager.

AM I TO SAVE, FIX OR PULL THE PLUG?

There are instances in which the only option is to terminate a project. The most obvious reason is when financial resources have been exhausted and there's no money to save, fix or complete a project. Also, anytime a project is affecting and endangering public safety, you must consider ending such a project. The main reason project management takes place is precisely so that the project gets completed. Salvaged projects brought to completion help stakeholders and they also help you become a better project manager. Therefore, work to rescue a project before you come to the conclusion to terminate it. Your final recommendation to stakeholders must be a professionally written statement listing your precise reasons for why the project is to be salvaged or terminated.

DEFINITION OF A SUCCESSFUL PROJECT

Is a pleased project owner enough of a reason to consider the project a success? Of course, it's not. If you hit the targets defined in your scope and the project is in absolute compliance with your budget and schedule, then you may correctly state that you have completed a successful project.

Relying on successful values, such as honesty, confidence, perseverance, integrity, innovation and adaptability, provides a solid base for success to rest upon. Celebrating your victories and embracing your challenges helps you learn and become better. These are also crucial factors to be included in your ever-changing formula for success.

Write your own definition of success and share it with the rest of the project's team. It will provide a clear target and allow for recognition and celebration when the team hits the bull's eye and the project's purpose is accomplished. Watch for the team and stakeholders saying "WOW" and use that as an indicator that success is surely on its way.

To create "WOW" experiences on all your projects, and to learn how the proper management techniques will create the "wow" factor everywhere, please visit www. TheBookonPM.com

PROJECT DELIVERY WITH A MISSION

Knowing the specific purpose for developing a project allows project management to revolve around a clear mission. A project manager who's aware of the main project's mission and understands the "What," "Why," and "Who" can easily focus resources around these reasons.

Make it part of your own personal practice to ask the project owner or sponsor, why this project? And do ask about the mission or main purpose for developing this project.

PROJECT MANAGEMENT BENEFITS YOUR BUSINESS PROFITABILITY

Learning to delegate responsibilities is an ability you develop once you fully comprehend, through extensive experience, what people can do for you and the project. Project managers are experts in understanding what each team member is responsible for and what each is capable of contributing to the progress and completion of the project.

Inexperienced project owners tend to delegate tasks to the inappropriate person or party. For example, they ask engineers questions meant for architects and ask architects to attend issues meant for a general contractor. During project management, simple mistakes cost money—a lot of money.

Money allows the project to start, then project management allows the project to move forward and, last, it allows for the completion of the project. It's a fact that money is truly the heart of the project and without it, the project may not survive. As you become more efficient and knowledgeable about reviewing and approving costs, your ability to reduce overspending by millions of dollars will increase. It will also allow your project management skills to benefit any organization financially.

To increase your business's bottom line and maximize profit, please visit www. TheBookonPM.com and schedule a professional consultation with an experienced project manager.

EVERY PROJECT IS UNIQUELY DIFFERENT

Even if you work in franchise project development and every project has the exact same requirements and goals, so they all look the same, the simple fact that the project is in a different location will make that project uniquely different. It's true, no two projects are alike, and as you recognize that every project has a unique set of rules and variables you'll begin to adapt to properly managing the differences in your projects.

Project management expands across several industries and is a profession practiced worldwide. Since scope for projects are diverse, procurement and team members are also diverse. It's like a meal using the exact same ingredients but cooked by different chefs; the taste and even the way the meal is served on the plate will be different. Subsequently, it's a smart practice to systemize your processes used during the project development to become more efficient and to allow repetition of tasks, so the parts of your process become automatic and predictable. In a way, the variables and differences in a project are what makes project management enjoyable. And, truthfully, your ability to handle the differences in diverse projects is what makes you a unique project manager.

A MEASURING STICK

How do you measure your project's success? There are many indicators to tell you that your project is going well and that you're being successful. For instance, a happy owner who's recommending you to other clients to the point that he already sold your services is a great sign that you're on the right track. Perhaps success shows up as passing every inspection with flying colors and earning the respect of inspectors. But for many people who trade their talent and time for money, the ultimate indicator for success comes via a significant bonus at the end of the year. You may have all or some of the previously mentioned indicators, but other important factors may not be present, such as the emotional well-being of the entire team. Moreover, there may be vendors who feel they were strategically obligated to do things outside their contract just to gain the opportunity to do business in future projects.

When half of the indicators aren't present and you receive an award, how would you feel about being recognized? On the other hand, if all indicators are there and no award is given, you'll probably feel blissful and accomplished.

It's nearly impossible to measure the true success of a project. You can't expect everybody to be completely satisfied, fully pleased and always preferring you as their project manager. Having stated this, how about outlining, during the planning process and scope definition, what would be considered a success for the project you're managing? This may give you a clear target that's easy to identify and a set of guidelines and expectations regarding the positive outcome of the project. Ask for and document a definition for success for your project in your detailed scope, vision, mission or your "goals documents." Then, work to get there.

CLOSE OUT

It's time to finalize all project activities and verify everything is completed across all phases. As you enter this phase and close the project to transfer the completed project as required the end of the road for the majority of your team members is near. You, as the project manager, have some critical and important steps to take before you sign off on the closing of all phases. During this phase it's critical to involve all project participants and stakeholders and use a robust checklist to make sure you cover each and every item that has been completed.

Soliciting feedback as you conduct a post-project survey is more opportunity to understand how the entire team feels about the project as a whole and in specific areas outlined in your survey. Including a "lessons learned" meeting allows you to gather useful information for the benefit and success of future projects. During this phase the collecting of project data to be archived is the actual deadline for the majority of the team members. If your project requires archives to comply with any regulations such as NARA (US National Archives and Records Administration) or others, verify that all submitted documents and data are in full compliance.

The checklist pertaining to your close out procedure may be extensive as every project has its own unique requirements and stakeholders often require specific information, such as financial audits. They may also have confidentiality requirements and may require disposal of sensitive information in order to properly close out a project. Ideally, your checklist for the close out phase is amended with every project you manage and it's your practice to always include a formal meeting with stakeholders prior to arriving at this particular phase.

USEFUL LIFE COSTS

For many developments, project management ends at the completion of a project, once the owner takes full control of the completed product. Infrequently, the project manager participates in managing the warranty period, typically lasting up to two years. Depending on the project delivery method, you may be asked to remain in the project since you are the official holder of the information pertaining to just about everything regarding the completed project.

If you're given the opportunity to participate in the management of a completed project, such as a building, while occupied by its end users you will get to see its operations and experience the maintenance phase. Thus, your ability to see the whole picture and have a better watchful eye during production will get sharper—since you'll have important knowledge about why things fail and need to be repaired during the two-year occupancy period (in the case of a building).

Always make the owner aware of the importance of performing a life cycle cost analysis, which simply means a complete understanding of total costs of ownership. Having the financial means to develop a project until the point of making it functional and operational is considered by most a healthy project budget. Eventually, the daily operational costs requirements of the building begin along with its demands for repairs and replacements. Often keeping up with expenses becomes such a big challenge that businesses are closed, buildings are abandoned or their functionality is limited.

To benefit from the services of an experienced project manager, please visit www. TheBookonPM.com and schedule a professional consultation.

SUSTAINABILITY

How long can anything be maintained at a certain rate or level? Even more specific, how long can a project sustain its healthy life while serving its intended function? And last, for how many years can it be sustained without undesirably impacting its surroundings or the environment?

The UN World Commission on Environment and Development definition for sustainability reads: "Sustainable development is development that meets the needs of the present without compromising the ability of future generations to meet their own needs." Now, since buildings require money to stay alive, let's look at financial sustainability. Imagine two people are sitting side by side and each of them have one dollar. The only way these two people may remain side-by-side is to give a dollar and then receive a dollar. So person "A" gives a dollar to person "B" at the same time person "B" gives a dollar to person "A." This process, as long as it happens precisely as described, can be sustained indefinitely. When there are multiple streams of income, including sophisticated systems for income generation coupled with a sound administration for all finances, your odds for remaining sustainable just increased.

Every project is to include the commonly avoided sustainability conversation since many project owners usually ignore it. Carefully bring this subject up and address its requirements. Working closely with all stakeholders, do your best to utilize the entire team's abilities. If you must, hire expert advice.

DECODE, DECRYPT AND DECIPHER

Documenting the entire process and creating a reliable system to access it, read it and understand it, may be one of the major challenges the project development industry faces. The information produced before, during and after a project in development is vast as it's inclusive of everything in relation to the entire life cycle of that project.

The main purpose for documenting a project is to have the ability to understand how, what, who, when and why things were developed in a certain way. There are many processes to organize, archive and access information, however no software out in the market does it all. Hence, you may be required to provide a hybrid solution to comply with project archiving and retrieval.

Make it a practice to document project information in a clear way so that

30 years from today, anybody who accesses the project database will be able to fully understand it.

A FINAL NOTE

Now, give yourself credit. Your project management knowledge, skills and tools have been complemented just by the mere fact you have read this book. Your journey as a project manager will be filled with amazing opportunities to leave this world a better place. Your participation in project management along with millions of fellow project managers around the globe will add to the efforts of the fastest growing profession in the world. Be efficient, honest and stay true to your values. Surprise yourself first, and every project you manage will become successful in every way, just as you imagined it. Share your story; spread the joy and your knowledge to those around you. You're already an amazing project manager. All that's left to do is for you to let it come out.

It is time to play! Enjoy your journey, as you may now efficiently and profitably perform project management.

Big Business Selling Strategies For Small Business Growth

GARY THOMPSON

The vast majority of small business owners, whether they offer a service or make and sell a product, are good at what they do. But, being wonderful at something doesn't automatically translate into being wonderful at selling or marketing it. Most small business owners lack the skills they need to manage successfully and grow their businesses, which is probably why so many of them fail during their first few years.

There are two key issues that are problematic. The first is that today, many small business owners come out of corporate environments. After 15, 18, or 20 years, they decide it's time to quit the proverbial rat race and start doing something they actually like, hopefully, love to do. If you're one of them, you know that it's scary at first. It's hard to get a new business off the ground, especially if you are used to being part of a team. In a small business, you're largely on your own, with no accounting, marketing, or sales department for support. It's all up to you.

So, you start wearing about 12 different hats, doing all kinds of tasks on your own, from cleaning the floors in the morning to shutting everything up in the evening. Instead of spending your day doing the one thing you started a business to do, you move from chore to chore. Plus, when you are that busy doing, you never have the time to think about marketing and growing your business.

Often, the hardest task you take on is salesperson because, at some point in the conversation, you have to talk about money. It's not necessarily difficult to share your passion for the business or talk about the wonderful things that your product or service does for the customer, but closing the sale and discussing the price can be truly uncomfortable. Even someone who has been in sales at another company can still feel some level of guilt about asking for an order at the retail price when it's for themselves. And that's a huge impediment to being an independent business owner. It's crucial to learn how to sell your product or service for what it — and you — are worth.

It's not a matter of garnering selling expertise or knowing what you know. Unfortunately, knowing isn't enough. You must also believe it, and believe in yourself. You need to understand and respect your own worth, as well as the worth of your product or service. If you can learn to sell without feeling like you are begging for money, then you can grow your business as opposed to just running that business.

Of course, first, you have to get to the point when you are running your company, not just working in it. Once you start generating more income by closing the sale more often, you will have the funds to start hiring people to handle the tasks that are diverting you from being a real owner. It's not as easy as sounds because, once you eliminate the classic excuse for not delegating ("I'd love to hire somebody, but I can't afford to"), it is time to face the underlying reasons why letting go of the little things is so difficult.

In many ways, this is more a personal decision than a business one in that the business reason is obvious: your time is worth more than what you would have to pay others to do the bookkeeping and buy the stationery supplies. The hard part is making the psychological shift that will allow you to trust other people to do as good a job as you can. If you can get over that hump just once, it will become easier each time you do it.

Coaching both corporate and small business clients has helped me codify a process for overcoming these all too common personal issues that keep people from realizing their full business or career potential. It starts with developing, cultivating and maintaining your sense of business-related worth, and then delivering the story of that worth in a compelling and believable manner. This chapter provides an overview of the five key things on which you will need to focus.

FIVE POWERFUL ELEMENTS TO LONG TERM BUSINESS GROWTH

1. Craft Your Story

The most important thing you need is your story, which means understanding who you are, what you stand for, why you are doing what you are doing and with whom you are looking to work. The key is focusing on the why. You may already be familiar with the best example of building and maintaining a compelling story, but it bears repeating because the Apple case study is excellent at making the point.

The company has done an extraordinary job, and it isn't necessarily because their products are any better than anybody else's. The company has an ethos, an approach that involves going well beyond the status quo, especially as it relates to customer service. In developing its story, Apple has given itself a huge advantage over other corporate cultures, one that draws people to the company. That advantage is the why, as in better customer service is the reason why to buy an Apple instead of a computer from one of its competitors.

A lot of small business owners lose or forget their why when they get involved in the day-to-day running of their companies. They forget why they are doing it, whatever it is, because they spend all their time actually doing it.

2. Create an Experience

Remembering your why helps you understand, envision and create the experiences your clients are going to enjoy from their interaction with you. Your product may work better than others of its kind, your customer service may be superior, the sales experience easier and so on.

3. Build a Narrative

Your narrative is a personalized version of what marketing experts call a positioning statement. It tells much of your story in that it puts forth a picture of who you are and what you're doing, and summarizes the benefits of being one of your clients. Since you are the one who will be telling your narrative, you need to feel comfortable with the words and the thoughts behind those words. You need to know and feel that you are telling the truth. It's important that the narrative you put out makes sure you're seen as the person you want to be, and that your customers' actual experiences support your narrative.

4. Be Selective

Trying to appeal to any and everyone is a marketing strategy that may work for large corporations with products that actually appeal to everyone, but it is a tragic mistake for small business owners. Think of it in terms of someone going door-to-door, trying to sell magazine subscriptions. That's basically what you're doing when you sit at your desk with a phone in your hand, calling a list of cold prospects. The same is true when you take the networking route, drop leaflets or run blanket advertising. The process is archaic and makes for extremely hard, time-consuming work. Worse still, it is soul destroying.

There are better ways of finding clients and customers, but they only work when marketing and sales genuinely work together. The concept of true cooperation between the two may feel foreign if you come out of the corporate world, where marketing and sales are separate entities somewhat in competition with each other. In fact, and the way it should work, marketing generates leads, and the salespeople convert them.

Your marketing efforts are to there to help people raise their hands and say "Yes, I'd like to talk to you." When there has been prior interaction with a lead who has self-identified themselves as interested in your product, the conversation is totally different than it is during a cold call. There is much less pressure put on you to justify the cost of your product, and that lessens or removes the guilt about discussing money. Distancing yourself from lead generation is also essential to better managing your time and your efforts. The time to step into the process is when a viable lead has been identified and engaged.

5. Know Your Numbers

When marketing and selling are working in tandem, you can trace the conversion process and its associated costs, from reaching someone and getting them to self-identify through to the final sale and the amount of that sale. Tracking these figures along with the lifetime value of a customer will allow you to determine how much it costs to acquire a new client or customer, as well as the value of an average customer. This will allow you to confidently set your marketing budget for attracting new customers and long-term growth.

IT'S EASIER WITH HELP

As discussed earlier in this chapter, most small business owners already find themselves trying to do it all on their own. Delegating some or all of the everyday activities can be a huge help in freeing up your time to begin rethinking the marketing and selling plan for your own company.

However, if you are like most people, you will soon see that there is a big difference between knowing what to do, understanding what activities go into doing it, and actually doing it on a regular basis. Everything in life takes a bit of a learning curve and enough practice on a regular basis so that you feel comfortable doing things in a different way. The process is the same for any new beneficial habit; you need to keep feeding it and watering it, much in the way you would water and feed a sprout until it becomes a healthy, growing plant.

The good news is that you don't have to go through the process alone. A good advisor can guide you through the learning curve and help you manage the time commitment involved so that you don't end up putting too much pressure on yourself. An advisor can also help you hold yourself accountable in terms of getting things accomplished. That's something that just about everyone struggles with in most areas of life, but especially so in business — and even more so when you are running and trying to grow your own business. Perhaps most importantly, a good advisor knows how to help you work through any of the "I'm not good enough" feelings and insecurities that affect just about everyone at some time.

If you would like to learn more about what goes into taking these five steps at Gary Thompson's Workshops, please visit www.ThatTallGuy.com

Branding Into Greatness

ANDRE DAWKINS

We all have greatness within us. The deciding factor is our will. Nothing that happens in life has any meaning unless we CHOOSE to make it so. Are you used to making quick decisions, or do you tend to procrastinate? Do you have strong will power? Do you act on emotion or on the thoughts you consciously choose? The answers to questions like these matter a great deal when it comes to greatness. Do you choose meanings consciously? Do you choose meanings that work for you instead of against you? Or do you react to situations based on emotion? Whatever you do, remember that you always achieve when you choose to put all your might into doing something good.

I'm a mortgage broker. A great one. It's why, if you're looking into investing in real estate, you should **CALL ANDRE at 1.647.991.7325.** Consider the following ...

- Instead of going to a bank for a home loan you can have me work on your behalf to both shop your rate with multiple lenders and manage your loan application from start to finish.
- Often times, when going to a bank directly to apply for a loan, you could instantly jeopardize your chance of approval by simply saying the wrong thing
- I can shop your rate for you at various banks. For example: Bank A may have the lowest mortgage rate available, Bank B may have the lowest closing costs available and Bank C may have the best combination of rate and fees.
- I'm your loan guide and can be very accessible and hands-on from start to finish, and I may find a home for your loan among my many lending partners, which is especially useful if you've been denied elsewhere. I can also provide more advanced/tailored recommendations or structure your loan favorably to lower costs.
- When it comes to your credit, I specialize in credit building and repairing, so I can provide you with a blueprint to get your credit on par.
- I can offer all types of home loans, from conventional options to non-conforming stuff. I typically offer a wide product choice because of my many partners.
- NOTE: like all other loan originators, I charge fees for my services. Additionally, I may get compensated from the lender I connect you with. But remember that I can offer competitive rates that meet or beat those of retail banks, so I should be considered alongside banks

when searching for financing. Typically, if you qualify at the bank and I arrange your mortgage, there will be no fees. I also have the ability to shop numerous lenders at once so I can find the best pricing based on your needs.

If the Bank says No ... **CALL ANDRE at 1.647.991.7325**

So the bank turns you down. This may seem like the end of the world, but it's not. There are many lenders out there, and I know a lot of them. Chances are with me to walk you through every step of the mortgage process, you'll find a home for your loan with one of my many partners. Here are some things you should know:

- All banks are not created equal. For example, every lender uses different policies and criteria when assessing your application— even if they're from the same parent company. I have access to this information and can match you up with a lender whose policies best suit your circumstances. To do this yourself, you'd have to go to each lender individually and assess their loan criteria and policies. Using me allows you to avoid this hassle and target the bank best suited to you.

- When you apply for a loan, it's crucial to realize that it will be registered on your credit file. This means you really don't want to shop around. You see, enquiries happen each time you apply for any kind of finance or credit (even entering a mobile phone contract) and can affect your ability to obtain credit in the future. Applying for loan after loan will actively destroy the likelihood that you'll ever be approved-- due to the number of enquiries building up on your credit file!

- Lenders don't like serial applicants, so rather than tackling a new loan application on your own, let me match you up with a suitable product first time around, to avoid this trap.

- Getting your ducks in a row. I'll be able to tell you what you can do to improve your chances of being approved for a loan—for example, waiting until you've been at your job a few more months before you apply, or closing the credit card with the large limit that's reducing your borrowing power.

- I'm also an expert in low-doc loans, perfect for those who are self-employed or have a hazy credit history. I'll even tell you exactly what paperwork is required, and how to get around any obstacles in the criteria set by different lenders.

- It's to my advantage to get you the best possible deal, as I want to maintain positive relationships with my lenders, thereby knowing I will never put you into a product you can't afford. My intention is to have nothing but happy clients that have only great things to say about the service they received from my team and myself, so they can refer their friends and family to have the same experience.

I'll also be hoping you give me a good review, as I build my business partly from referrals—so it's always in my best interest to do the best thing by you.

By working with me, you could secure yourself a loan with a much lower interest rate or bonus features, potentially saving you tens of thousands of dollars over the life of the loan. Whether you're an investor or a homebuyer, if you would like further information and guidance about securing finance after your bank has said no, **CALL ANDRE at 1.647.991.7325.**

WHY YOU NEED A MORTGAGE BROKER

- They're mortgage experts who provide different lenders, loan types and rates for buyers without upfront charges.

- They can offer loan and rate options that a traditional bank may not be able to.
- They gather and manage critical paperwork while coordinating loan information with relevant parties.
- They help create your loan and close your home buying transaction properly.
- They typically close on your home faster than a traditional bank.
- You're not locked into working with a mortgage broker, and if for any reason they're not providing exceptional service, you can change brokers.

MARKET AWARENESS ... IN TERMS OF HOW BRANDING HAS ALLOWED ME TO STAND OUT IN THE MARKETPLACE.

When I first started doing mortgages, it was a constant struggle. It felt like everywhere I would turn there was doubt and closed doors. It felt as if I would never see success in this industry at all.

I keep telling myself, there has got to be a way, I gave my all to carve a niche into the marketplace. It all spiraled from the moment I adopted the principle slogan "if the bank says NO WAY? Better Call Andre!" It felt as if immediately a lightbulb went off in the consumers' eyes. Now, I'm not saying that all of a sudden everyone came running to me, however, the point is with the brand evolution it created an arena for me to play in. Once I came to the realization that I had something positive here, I immediately began my quest to build brand awareness through marketing.

I first started doing door to door hand outs of flyers that I would bring to a selected area. I was on a shoestring budget and had to make it because my "Y or why" was bigger than my how. I didn't know how it was going to happen, but I knew why it needed to happen. I was fed up with mediocrity, so I began visualizing myself as being successful. I began envision the life I wanted to create through the funnelling of my mortgage business. Then I applied my foot on the gas and keep it moving. Fast forward, I am constantly working on building and evolving my brand awareness. I was once told, closed mouths don't get fed. That hit home, as I came to realize the more the market knows of your existence, then the more the market can come to you for support and service.

I stand on the principles that I am here to serve, care for and change the lives of all my clients and customers—one deal at a time.

The moment I started making sales, I reinvested into marketing. I was fortunate to be working a full time job and earning a handsome salary. Therefore, all the mortgage money I made went right into advertising. I first put an ad in a local newspaper called SHARE newspaper, then later I put an ad on a local radio station G98.7 FM. To date, I still advertise in those two mediums because it was that foundation which allowed me to have such great market penetration.

The best part is I am only warming up. I plan to become a household name where "Call Andre" becomes a brand that is well recognized by the public.

Be on the lookout for the CA Mortgage Group: we will be expanding the brand into a more user-friendly platform from a standpoint of other agents using the Call Andre systems and techniques to serve, care for and change the lives of their customers. This is so they don't have to say I'm a mortgage agent/broker at the Call Andre Mortgage Group. The sound of CA Mortgage Group will be more appealing. But don't get confused: Call Andre is here to stay. The brand, the focus, the mission, the greatness … We are here to serve.

THINGS THE BANK WON'T TELL YOU

- You don't need a high credit score to qualify for a loan. If you're under the impression that you need a 720 credit score or higher to score the home of your dreams, think again. Many mortgage lenders require a minimum score of 680 to secure a loan. If you are applying for a High Ratio (insured mortgage with less than 20% down) mortgage loan, you may even qualify with a score of 600.

- Banks claim to have the best interest rates and have your best interest at heart, so how come it is that if you go to your bank to get a mortgage, they quote you a rate? They don't give you the best rate from the beginning. Why is it that you have to then re-approach them with a competitor rate to get them to match it.

- They usually have hidden clauses in their products that they do not inform you of. For example, a collateral charge ... where they register a higher amount on the title than the actual mortgage you are getting. In other words, they hold your equity hostage.

- The penalties to break your mortgage with a big bank are a lot higher than some of the same "A" lending institutions that mortgage brokers can get you into, and they are federally regulated just like a bank. They are called monoline lenders; monoline because they only have one line of business and that, of course, is mortgages. So they will not try to cross sell you and ultimately try to sink you in more debt.

- Fees and rates vary between lenders. Don't be afraid to shop around a little bit before deciding on a mortgage lender. Typically, each lender charges different origination fees and closing costs. While it may only be 5% of the purchase price of your home, that's a big chunk of change. Search for the best deal to save yourself as much money as possible.

- Closing at the end of the month is always better. If you choose to set your closing date at the beginning of the month, you'll end up paying more "prepaid interest," which is due at closing. Set your closing date as close to the end of the month as you can to avoid paying extra upon settling.

- Longer term mortgages cost more. If you talk to any mortgage lender, they'll try to push you towards a 30-year loan. You may think that this is because it's more affordable for you. While it will cost you less on a month-to-month basis, you'll end up paying quite a bit more in interest. If you can swing the extra money, shoot for a 15- or 20-year mortgage instead.

- There are ways to take a break from your mortgage payments. When times get tough and you are struggling to make your mortgage payment, you do have options beyond foreclosure and short sales. Most lenders offer skip-a-payment or forbearance options for those who qualify. Depending on the severity of your situation, you may even be eligible to have your payments suspended for a few months.

- Don't fall for gimmicks. Even if a lender advertises a no-cost closing, there's usually a catch. Depending on the circumstances, the lender may roll the closing costs into the loan. This means that you're actually paying more for the closing costs over the life of the loan due to interest. If it's not rolled into your loan, they may charge a higher interest rate—which would also cost you more over time.

- Most of the front line staff that you and the clients are dealing with are not home owners themselves and cannot provide you with a great scope of knowledge and information because they can't speak to you from experience. They are only trained to sell you the products the bank has to offer.

CREDIT

I Specialize in credit building and repairing. Credit to me is the most important aspect of a mortgage transaction. There are three vital parts when it comes to residential lending... the property, the credit and the income. You must have two out of three working for you to get an approval.

Credit is something that needs to be branded into every student's head before they leave elementary school. In my opinion it should be taught in grade eight. The reason being is not all students end up finishing high school. However, most kids tend to complete elementary. I think that if the average Canadian was taught how important credit is throughout their whole adult life, we would have a lot less people in a position with bad credit.

It hurts my inner being when I see someone with bruised credit, especially when they are for little issues (i.e. unpaid bills, late payments, etc.).

The biggest negative effect on one's credit is usually phone bills, as most people don't realize that yes, they are reported to your credit bureau.

If you are in a rough position, of being one of the unfortunate, misguided individuals who has been plagued by the credit system. give me a call and let's discuss your situation. There are still options available to you. Believe it or not, like insurance, everyone is entitled to a mortgage. However, just like auto insurance, you pay higher premiums when your records are bad. With mortgages you pay higher rates and higher fees when your credit is bad.

I often times advertise "No job, no credit, your approved!" This is another one of my many brand slogans, however, oftentimes, people think this applies to institutional mortgages. That is clearly not the case: the only time this is applicable is with a private mortgage.

When people approach me for a mortgage, the first thing I tell them to do is pull their credit report themselves then gather the required docs, so that we can review and work out a game plan… its beyond me to know the rate of people that stop the process, simply because they feel like I am making them do too much work. My mentor once told me, anything worth having is worth working hard for… so I empower you to follow my instructions, so we can build your financial future and make your dreams of homeownership a reality.

TEAM WORK

No man is an island… I plan on adopting this principle. I am so used to being a workaholic technician that it shows up in my brand "Call Andre." Hence the reason for the brand evolution into "CA Mortgage Group." We will re-engage that marketplace and bring awareness to the community, letting them know that Call Andre is now team, a force that is to be reckoned with, as we will stand together to serve and care for our clients, changing their lives one deal at a time.

I believe team work is important in all aspects of life, especially in the real estate market place. If you think about it, when you purchase a home, you have many people on your side working with you to get you from point A – Z. Your team consists of your mortgage broker, your realtor, your lawyer, your home inspector, your home appraiser and your financial planner

It's always good to make sure you have the best players on your side working on your best interest at all times. They should have one common goal: to serve and care for your needs and to make your experience an exceptional one. That is what we strive for here at **Call Andre at 1.647.991.7325.**

Unstoppable

The Art of Striving

DEREK G. CHAN

HOW TO BE UNSTOPPABLE

It has been said that in order to obtain a goal, one must first see it in the mind. The child who decides he wants a cookie from the jar that's high up on the shelf or the person who wants to make partner in the law firm where they now work—each uses the same mechanism or mindset. They understand at a visceral level that you become what you think about.

The difference between the student who can break boards with their hands and feet and the one who can't, isn't skill—it's all mindset, the belief, the deep-seated knowledge that one can do it.

Golf is an interesting game. The person who can best remember the components of a good swing AND can also envision them is the one who will hit the ball far, true and straight. So it is with martial arts: you must develop a set of beliefs or a mindset that will allow you to become unstoppable. Your approach needs to be holistic in nature.

Definition of Holistic: relating to or concerned with wholes or with complete systems rather than with the analysis of, treatment of, or dissection into parts

- Holistic medicine attempts to treat both the mind and the body
- Holistic ecology views humans and the environment as a single system

At Ko Fung Martial Art, we train body, mind and soul, integrating the three elements into a holistic mindset that will make you unstoppable in life.

One of my students, Lesia Rogers, had this to say about our "wellness" approach:

Sifu Derek has truly been a blessing to me, and I am extremely grateful. It has been a year this month since he took me under his wing to teach me how first to love myself. I've also been given many tools through martial art training, coaching and nutrition.

When I first started with Derek, I was already training with someone in Tai Chi, but I'd always wanted to learn self-defence and was looking for a different martial art. Interestingly, the first thing Derek coached me to do was slow down, something I still struggle with to this day.

In the beginning, I was extremely scared and hesitant, but Derek maintained a strong awareness and was always sensitive to my needs. This was important to me as I am an emotional person and needed to reset my mindset to love, acceptance, trust, building confidence and not being afraid of life. He spent hours with me and was by my side through the thick and thin of my life (my accomplishments and my

140

challenges). It has not been an easy journey.

I learned that it takes time for change to happen, that it requires belief in ourselves, and through coaching and training Derek has given me the beautiful gift of awareness of who I really am and what I really want in life. He's made me realize anything is possible if I truly want it. For example, I spent five years with other trainers struggling with little change in my WEIGHT. The first thing Derek did was teach me about mindset to help me understand what it takes to achieve my weight loss goal. By slowing down, listening, AND DOING, I was able to lose 10 pounds in less than two months.

Most recently he has taught me that we often face challenges in life that we have no control over. With the sudden loss of my husband, he has taught me by being there for me that life must go on. In fact, if it wasn't for Derek in the past year, I wouldn't have been prepared to deal with this sudden loss and the corresponding changes in my life.

Change is very scary and can happen suddenly. Although nobody is ever really prepared for tragedy, we must move on and take back control of our lives. Derek has been very supportive and has taught me about acceptance, redirecting and letting go with everything we do in life.

I am a stronger person than I was a year ago when we first started. Thank you to Derek. I know I would be worse off without his coaching.

I had no idea how disciplined martial art can be until I met Derek and learned his way of life. And even though I am now alone (we are never really alone), I am beginning to fill the empty space within by learning to be by myself and love myself truly.

Grateful for every moment and every breath I take, thank you, Sifu Derek.

As mentioned, martial arts represent a pathway to developing a mindset that allows you to be unstoppable. I'll provide a holistic approach to developing this mindset in your own life and give you the tools to deal with hard times whenever you encounter them. You'll learn about martial arts principles and how to apply them to your daily living. Being unstoppable is not about fearlessness or strength, but about recognizing fear and still moving forward.

In training, a martial artist gets used to regular defeats and, in turn, sees them as an opportunity to learn. Tou Lou (martial art routine) or the forms in martial arts teaches us progression. One sequence of movements leads to another. You must learn each fundamental movement first before you can move to the next sequence of movements. This structured type of learning and milestone-based achievement is valuable in all aspects of life.

Wing Chun, in particular, is an effective tool to prepare those who practice it for real life. It does so by developing skills necessary for when one encounters difficult situations. Its concepts and principles are particularly enlightening when properly interpreted and digested under a good Sifu's guidance. Form in the Wing Chun system teaches the practitioner—Awareness, Body Structure, Balance, Body Mechanics and Relaxation. Technique drills or single drills in the Wing Chun system teach the individual how to use those principles during a confrontation.

An essential aspect of having an unstoppable mindset is the ability to make timely decisions in stressful and ambiguous situations. A decision may be either right or wrong, but it's crucial to remember that far worse than an incorrect decision is a situation where no decision is made when one is necessary. Through a variety of cooperative and semi-cooperative drills, a Wing Chun practitioner is able to develop intuition, reflexes and decision-making skills while under pressure.

An example of a Wing Chun drill that develops these skills is the famous 'Chi Sao' (sticking hand) training. It is a two-person tactile sensitivity drill. One only does the attacking while the other is only defending. The objective of the attacker is learning how to use leverage, distance, angle and openings to create a successful attack. At the same time, the defender is learning how to maintain proper body structure, relaxation and counter movements while under pressure with unplanned attacks. The key to Chi Sao is accepting the force coming in (relaxation) instead of using force against force.

This develops decision-making skills through checking assumptions against facts, and develops problem-solving skills by making its practitioners consider the possible impact of their decisions throughout the process of the drill. This gives the two practitioners an opportunity to test their strengths and weakness while promoting unique and unplanned learning processes to occur.

POWER OF BREATH - STRESS MANAGEMENT

A crucial concept in Wing Chun is that of proper breathing. Siu Nim Tao is the first open hand form from the Wing Chun system and is a form of breathing meditation. Siu Nim Tao translates to "Little Idea," meaning everything starts with a thought. Without proper breathing, movement becomes stilted and ineffective. Proper abdominal breathing is a skill that is crucial for a healthier and stronger body and also for focus, which is why it is one of the first things taught.

In addition to the health and training benefits of breathing, it can also be used as an important tool for stress management. Breathing has both voluntary and involuntary control mechanisms. You can shift from being its pilot to allowing it to be left on autopilot. The voluntary aspect of breathing is what allows us to tap into its stress-managing potential.

Breathing exercises act as a form of meditation in Chinese Martial Arts. Proper abdominal breathing used in this type of meditation allows a greater volume of breath and leads to a decrease in activity of stress markers and blood levels of stress hormones.

Oftentimes, when our life is stressed, the integrity of our automatic breathing suffers. Taking advantage of the control we can exert on breathing allows us to combat stress. Learning to control our breathing can allow us to begin to control other parts of our body as well. The mind-body connection developed through breathing exercises not only physically improves our breathing but can also increase self-awareness. When you bring your body and mind in tune, your mental state will be much improved, and less susceptible to stress.

BODY STRUCTURE

Martial arts teach the skills of how to use your body structure to your advantage, and offers understanding on how the body's structure works in terms of structural alignment, the linkage of the joints, and also how simple geometry and physics can be applied to the body. A central focus of Wing Chun is adopting particular stances and postures as a framework from which to launch attacks and counter-attacks. Doing this without good posture will greatly limit your ability to be effective. In fact, your Wing Chun techniques won't be as effective unless your body is aligned correctly. This alignment also reinforces the important concept of breathing and can directly impact your ability to draw and use your breath.

Good posture means that the body is aligned with gravity, walks tall and moves with freedom in the joints. Posture in martial arts is vitally important.

This is the reason most martial arts emphasize structure from the beginning. Physical structure from a Kung Fu point of view involves a little more than just good posture, though. In addition to good posture, it adds internal connections such that your entire body learns to move as a single fluid and powerful unit.

The efficient way to get a feel for a student's structure is through single drills, Chi Sao and sparring. Good structure can be almost invisible—even to the trained eye. However, the lack of it can usually be felt as soon as contact is made with your opponent. If an opponent has good structure, a lot of techniques you could try are unlikely to work, but if their structure is poor or non-existent, almost anything you do will be effective.

What exactly is good structure and why is it so important? To put it in simple terms, good structure is the way in which you connect the different parts of yourself together internally so that they are aligned with the forces acting on your body. In Wing Chun principle and theory, the curves of the spine should be aligned, eliminating as much curvature as much as possible. It's done by tucking in the chin backward and slightly scooping forward the tailbone to avoid an anterior pelvic title. Shoulders should be relaxed and dropping with the body. By doing so, the body is able to absorb and deliver a force as one bodily unit.

The majority of people are completely disconnected and don't have proper alignment and coordination with their body. Their arms will do one thing, their legs something different, with hips only being vaguely involved. When the body does so many different things, it's impossible to connect the breath or the mind to what it's doing. This results in internal chaos and a feeling that you lack the resources to cope with your physical situation. The truth is, you don't lack the resources at all; you've just scattered them. The key to good structure is in learning how to gather all the parts of yourself together so that you can put everything you are into everything you do.

Good structure connects your arms and legs together through your centre and involves your breath working in harmony with your movements. Most importantly, the whole process is controlled by your mind, which stays focused on what you're doing. When you're connected internally, every movement involves your whole body. This internal structure can easily be felt. For example, when you try to move someone's arm who is well connected internally, you can feel that in trying to move their arm you are moving the weight of their whole body.

RELAXATION

Relaxation is a great example taught in martial arts that can easily be applied to everyday life. To be relaxed is to be natural. It should be like pouring water into your cup without any muscle tension. To get a better understanding of how to apply this in daily life, we remember how relaxation, in the context of martial arts, is supposed to be understood.

When I teach Wing Chun, I like to begin by emphasizing to my students that, in training, techniques are performed in a relaxed manner. This occurs both during training and in actual combat. In order to develop force, one must be able to relax. Why? The equation for force is mass multiplied by acceleration, and if there's any sort of muscle tension, it will only slow down the acceleration. I tend to use an analogy of a car. In order for a car to move smoothly, you will have to step on the accelerator. Step on the brake and accelerator at the same time, and it will feel like you're getting a lot of power, but in reality, you're not going anywhere.

If the arm is tensed, maximum punching speed cannot be achieved. To begin a punching motion, the arm must, in essence, first be relaxed. If relaxed at the onset, the punching may begin at any time. It is a fact that one motion is always faster than two. If there is unnecessary tension, energy will be wasted, and this will, in turn, create fatigue. In an extended engagement, this can be critical. Tension stiffens your body and thus reduces your ability to sense and react to your opponent's intentions. Look at the sport of boxing. The best boxers don't get tired—even after 12 rounds. A huge part of this is that they don't waste energy on inefficient movement. Less experienced boxers may look good early in a fight, but they often crumble in the later rounds due to not being relaxed.

I will now paraphrase two of the core points of this lesson:
1. **Tense muscle slows down your reaction speed.**
2. **Unnecessary tension wastes energy, causing fatigue.**

If you're overcome by anger or are tense, your mind faces identical effects and, consequently, you'll have difficulty acting with the speed you need. This unnecessary tension in your mind doesn't only waste your energy and time, it also creates a lot of undesired situations that will now need to be solved. A person with a relaxed mind can always see things more clearly than a quick-tempered person. Thus, they can easily react with proper speed and attitude. This is why a person who understands the principle of relaxation correctly can certainly be more careful and successful; they react only when necessary by keeping calm and relaxed.

BALANCE

Balance is important to all martial arts, and especially Wing Chun. It's a concept that ties together both relaxation and structure. Without balance you can't maintain structure, nor can you be relaxed as you'll always be fighting to adjust yourself and the structure you've moved away from.

The Merriam-Webster dictionary defines balance as follows:

bal·ance noun \ba-lən(t)s
- The state of having your weight spread equally so that you do not fall
- The ability to move or to remain in a position without losing control or falling
- A state in which different things occur in equal or proper amounts or have an equal or proper amount of importance

Balance in Kung Fu is often associated with the physical sense of the word. I teach my students from the day they walk in how to understand their bodies in order to develop the balance necessary to perform the forms and techniques in Wing Chun. However, physical balance isn't the only form of balance a martial arts student should learn to hone. Balance in Wing Chun isn't only about your own physical body, but understanding how to create balance between two individuals. The highest level in the art of Wing Chun isn't about how to destroy or how to inflict the most pain in an individual, but how to neutralize and balance an opponent's incoming force without harming them, and at the same time preventing them from hurting you.

"The best battle is the one that has not been fought."
- Sun Tzu

This is one of the other reasons why in Wing Chun we'll focus heavily on Chi-Sao, as it helps us understand how to find balance between two individuals—either by changing to a different position or stepping in a different angle. This is one of the skills that's transferable to everyday life and relationship-building.

There is a saying that Wing Chun Kung Fu is easy to learn but hard to master. One reason is that, in the Wing Chun system, there's a fine balance between each movement and technique. Each movement needs to be precise. There can't be any gray area as it could be a matter of your life or death in a physical confrontation. In order to find the fine balance, though, one must understand not what to do but what not to do.

Understanding this concept will also help you find balance with your overall well-being and health. It's not about knowing what type of workout we should be doing or what type of food we should eat, but what we should not be doing or eating on a daily basis. Example: all rigorous physical activity can wear down the body, and you can feel tired, sore or injured. One must always balance training and rest, and in the case of an injury, you must listen to your body. Training when too fatigued or coming back too soon from an injury can set your training back by keeping you out even more in the long run.

ROOTING AND CENTRALIZATION

"When you have roots there is no reason to fear the wind."
- Chinese Proverb

In order to understand how to become unstoppable in classical martial arts training you must recognize that it all begins with the foundation. So what does the foundation include? Strengthening the lower body by lowering your center of gravity and widening up your base. Learning how to align your skeletal structure at the same time as relaxing your body. If we're able to be rooted to the ground and our body is up straight, it's most likely going to be harder to be pushed out of balance. You can try this when you are taking the bus or subway.

1. **Imagine your head is being slightly pulled up.**
2. **Widen your base (knees are a shoulder width apart).**
3. **Slightly bend your knees to lower your center of gravity.**

You'll automatically feel more balanced and centered. A solid base is required in order for you to grow your skills and techniques. It's the same in life. It's important to understand what keeps you grounded, to discover both your values and your beliefs. By doing so, you're able to hold your ground no matter what conditions life gives you.

By being grounded, you'll eliminate fear and find inner peace. This happens as you gain the courage and strength to overcome whatever fears you might have. Training in the martial arts will always push you to your limits. It tests not only your physical strength but your mental strength as well. Know this: each time you're ready to give up, you're facing a true test of willpower. You push yourself to the limit to see how much more you can take and to see how much more you're willing to go through in order to achieve your goal. This mental strength develops into an unbreakable warrior spirit, giving you the courage to persevere through your darkest hours.

ACCEPTANCE AND LETTING GO

At a certain point in your training the ability to 'let go' becomes essential. The concept of letting go functions on two levels—physical and mental. To be able to truly let go, the physical, mental (includes emotional) aspects must function in unison.

Physically you learn to relax and release your muscles, tendons and ligaments. When you do this, it leads to the deepening of one's root and the ability to ground a powerful incoming force. In terms of meditation, this means relaxing as much as possible and 'trusting' the Earth to hold you up.

The emotional and mental aspects of 'letting go' are intertwined, meaning that emotions can trigger thought patterns, and certain thought patterns can trigger emotions. You should look for evenness and balance in your emotion. This is a non-reactive state rather than an absence of emotion per se. This emotional neutrality is like a placid lake that appears to be a mirror. In this state, it becomes possible to read a person's true emotional intention like an open book.

For the mind, you want, at first, a gentle calmness and a slowing of thought, but this eventually develops into what has been termed 'mind of no mind.' This mind of no mind is actually an optimal state for both the meditative aspect as well as the martial. For meditation, we can perceive and become aware of things without the mind's judgement. In martial arts, this 'mind of no mind' state is optimal for success in combat. When centered in such a state you are able to act or react at a speed that can be faster than the speed of thought!

Accepting and letting go are probably two of the hardest things to do. Whether it's a relationship, anger from an argument or simply past mistakes; instead of being stuck in the moment, accept the emotion and the situation with your arms wide open. Acknowledge, embrace and let go. Let go of emotions and situations that don't serve you as a whole or lead you to greater things. It's beyond whether you were right or wrong. It's about setting yourself free. It begins with the willingness to accept ourselves exactly as we are, right where we are, with no judgements or preconceived notions. For the martial element, you must go even further. Instead of fearing an opponent's attack, you must learn to welcome it. This is all a matter of lack of tension. Therefore, the stronger an attack, the more relaxed you must initially become to deal with it. This method is grounded in a Wing Chun principle that states, "Accept what comes, escort what leaves." By accepting the incoming force, it will enable you to reposition and let go of what's coming in at you.

Once this is accomplished you no longer react to circumstances as average people do. Instead, you find yourself centered and alert—ready to deal with a situation without having your natural adrenal reaction getting in the way. This is not only supremely useful in combat but also in your daily life.

MOVING FORWARD

"Your one-step back is your opponent's two-step forward."
–Derek G. Chan

One of the most important rules of Wing Chun is that you don't step back. It is structure that gives us the advantage over the larger opponent, and when we become our worst enemy by destroying our own structure, it's not too difficult to predict the outcome of a fight. While Wing Chun may have backward stepping and backward bracing, these footworks are not designed for you to initiate. In Wing Chun we always move forward; only when the force dictates it do we actually move backwards. Footwork in Wing Chun is always taking you forward. It might be in a direct straight line or at an angle, but it allows you to swallow up any space that opens up between you and an attacker, limiting their options and overwhelming them.

Some of the most skilful boxers are those that can deliver a knockout blow while going backwards. While this may be much to the appreciation of the crowd, Wing Chun has no time for any of this. The footwork drives you forward all the time. One of the most important rules I always remind my students of during our sparring sessions is to continue to move forward—mentally and physically. It's important to create opportunities either by footwork, by stepping in a different angle, or a follow-up technique. There may be times when it is best to be stationary and wait for the perfect timing and openings. However, if you are against a more experienced opponent, the only chance of you overcoming the situation is by closing the distance and creating the opening. If you don't, not only do you have a lesser chance of winning, you're also leaving yourself vulnerable as a stationary target.

By having the attitude of forward movement, it will greatly benefit you in your daily life. Life is your experienced and stronger opponent. It doesn't matter how organized or how well-planned you are; life will always throw obstacles at you. In order for you to conquer them, you must start by moving forward. If you keep waiting for the perfect time or the perfect day, you'll never get anything done, and, sadly, you'll also miss a lot of opportunities. Instead, start moving forward and create your own path, regardless of how tough the situation is. If there's a will there is a way.

FOCUS

It can take a continuous daily effort to reach your goals. However, focusing on your long-term expectations, you'll find the strength to keep going even in the face of temporary setbacks. Those trained in Wing Chun will tell you that in the process you'll face a lot of challenges and setbacks. The students who are able to recognize that such setbacks are necessary hurdles and pitfalls they must navigate along the path to their destination are also the ones who succeed. Without that realization a student faces great difficulty overcoming those setbacks because they may lose sight of their long-term goals and allow themselves to get lost, joining the many casualties who fall by the wayside.

To focus, you must not only find a goal but also envision and look beyond at what lies ahead. The same principle applies to Karate practitioners when they attempt to break boards. If they only focus on the surface, their success rate of breaking the boards decreases as their force will be slowed down before they reach the target. However, if they are envisioning and telling themselves to hit behind or through the boards, the chance of them breaking the board is a lot higher.

Life is a series of experiences. There will be times where you're stuck in the moment. Whether it's a failure in a business partnership or the loss of a family member, it's up to you to endure and envision what lies ahead and continue to march forward. By doing so, you'll develop a stronger self and character. This is what separates those who are short-sighted from those who are long-sighted.

TECHNIQUE—EFFICIENT AND ECONOMICAL

"Offence is Defence, Defence is Offence."
- Wing Chun Proverb

One of Wing Chun's unique points is that it doesn't rely on any brute strength to overcome an adversary. We'll always place ourselves as the fragile person. Why? There will always be someone bigger, stronger and faster. And the way to overcome a larger assailant is by understanding the power of proper body structure and relaxation.

To become more efficient and economical with your movements, you'll defend and attack simultaneously. Doing so will allow you to become more efficient with your movements. One example is the Lap Da or Lap Sao technique. This is a technique where one hand sinks the opponent's straight attack while your other hand punches. In order to execute these fine movements, there will be an emphasis on body coordination drills. Without being coordinated, you wouldn't have the ability to execute the technique as smoothly. Wing Chun techniques often require you to have your hands and lower body cooperating with one another. Being well coordinated also means one is well-balanced. As human beings, we already apply the principle of balance while we are walking, our left hand will swing out, right foot steps forward, and vice versa. However, as a martial artist sometimes we tend to forget about this basic principle, and we think martial arts movements and everyday movements are two separate entities.

Having the Wing Chun mindset of being efficient will change our approach to handling daily tasks. It will help us realize how important it is to utilize our energy more efficiently (as it will help us manage time). In Wing Chun philosophy, time is an important factor. For this reason, each movement and technique has to be precise. As it could be a matter of life or death if you're in a confrontation. Every inch, every angle, every movement comes into play. Wing Chun is a system that does not discriminate, as it is not about who is bigger, stronger and faster. It's about understanding how to utilize proper body mechanics and physics to your advantage. It's understanding how to execute the most impactful thing efficiently and effectively in the limited time and energy you're given. This is why, in classical martial arts, you'll strike on vital spots and soft tissues on the opponent when placed in a life or death situation. By embracing this Wing Chun concept, you're able to focus more and utilize your time and energy more efficiently and effectively in your regular daily routine.

To learn more about Derek's method of Wing Chun visit us at
www.kofung.ca or contact us at info@kofung.ca

Never Give Up!

My Journey to Purpose

VIVIAN STARK

NEVER GIVE UP: GROWTH AND SUCCESS COME IN INCREMENTS, NOT LEAPS

My desire is to encourage you with my life story. I have spent my life learning and improving myself, and I am thrilled to share what I have learned with you. Today I am living my definition of success. I have said NO TO THE PITY PARTY! Personal growth and development are a daily diet staple, and have fueled me in my business and entrepreneurial successes.

I wake up every day, knowing I am living my life with purpose, knowing I am the kind of person I always wanted to be. I have faced many challenges; my story has failures as well as successes. But I have learned that setbacks are only a part of the story; they are not the whole story. The story keeps going as long as you keep trying. You can choose to quit and make the story end in failure or dissatisfaction, or you can choose to keep trying and make your story what you want it to be.

Never give up. Success and growth do not come in leaps, they come in increments. The challenges will keep coming at you and sometimes it feels like two steps forward, one step back. But remember you did have those steps forward and you will again – if you never give up. You can choose to be overcome by dreck that life throws at you, or you can open your eyes to the love and opportunity that are always there too. You can have the life you want if you never, never, never give up on what is important – You.

IT IS YOUR LIFE - LIVE IT YOUR WAY

My life is my own for the making, but I did not always know this. I lived a very sheltered life as a child, fiercely protected by my overbearing Greek parents. I was not allowed to do the 'normal' girl things, like have sleepovers or join the Girl Guides to be a Brownie. When I was older I was not allowed to date for fear of gossip within my community. My parents lived in fear of the unknown. I lived in fear of being reprimanded if I disobeyed.

Despite my fear, insecurity, and extremely introverted personality, I pushed myself to exert my independence and fulfill certain goals that I set out for myself. From a very young age, I felt that I always needed to prove myself. To prove that I was pretty enough, smart enough, or even good enough. I worked tirelessly to achieve my dreams, never sharing them with anyone for fear of being ridiculed.

I began pursuing my goals as a young teen who wanted to fit in. I lived in an affluent area of Vancouver and always felt out of place. I did not have all the cool clothes that everyone else had, so I worked with my brother as a gardener cutting grass for one of my dad's clients. I saved my money and bought the clothes I wanted so that I would 'fit in' with the crowd. Despite this, I never felt that I fit in with other kids.

I was a rather "ugly duckling" as a younger girl, with a massive overbite and awkward shyness about me. After having braces, I felt my "ugly" stage was behind me and I decided to take a modeling class over several weeks one summer when I was in high school. My parents did not support me in this decision, so I chose to pay for it myself. The modeling class cost $800. I worked at Zellers for $3.00/hour. I persevered and saved enough money to pay for the class.

It turns out that the modeling class was just what I needed. I learned how to carry myself and exude confidence. After finishing the class, I took several modeling jobs and had many successes in my short modeling career. I made the cover of the then prestigious Back to School catalog for Eaton's Department Store, along with several other fun and exciting modeling adventures.

My modeling highlight and a fond memory was when I was hired for a ski catalog. (They wanted a curvy model. Who knew that sometimes it pays to not be super skinny!) We were taken up to the top of Blackcomb Mountain by helicopter before the official ski season opening. I remember having to jump out of the helicopter into three feet of snow because the helipad was snow-covered, and the helicopter could not land. I was paid $850 per day for three days. It was a dream come true. I felt validated.

When I was nineteen I began dating a handsome Greek guy I met at a wedding. Before I knew it, his parents and my parents got together and began planning our wedding. I literally cannot remember him actually asking me to marry him. How sad is that? Some time before our wedding I found out that he was into drugs and was still seeing his ex-girlfriend. I broke up with him and cancelled the wedding.

To escape well-meaning friends and relatives, I took an extended holiday to Greece where I could recover from the breakup. Armed with my modeling composite cards and my lovely, fashionable clothes, I hoped to land some modeling jobs while I was there. Instead, I met another handsome Greek guy who was smooth and charming. He swept me off my feet.

In classic old-school Greek fashion, my mom flew to Greece to check him out and determine whether he was a suitable partner for me. Like I said, I lived a sheltered life. She approved and, after a civil wedding in Canada, I moved to Greece to start my life with my new husband.

The first thing he did when we settled in to our home was give away all my beloved clothes. He proceeded to tell me what I could and could not do, where I could and could not go, and how I had to act. He, like my parents, was consumed with what other people thought of him and now me. I was terrified. What had I done?

I realized very quickly I had made a huge mistake and wanted to leave him and go back to Canada. To my surprise, I was already pregnant. Too embarrassed to tell anyone my sad state of affairs, I stayed in Greece. I had made an agreement with my husband that our children would be born in Canada. I did not want to risk my children having to go to the army if they were boys. After my first son was born, I returned to Greece.

When I became pregnant with my second son, I decided to leave Greece, not to return. I told my husband I was going back to Canada and he could come with me or not. He chose to move to Canada with me, but we broke up after a few years. Our marriage was just not meant to be, but I was blessed with two healthy, adorable and rambunctious boys that I loved so much.

Once divorced, my husband went back to Greece to avoid paying child support and to be near his momma, so she could pamper and take care of him. (It's a Greek thing. He was a huge momma's boy. Never again.) I was determined that my two boys would never be momma's boys!

THE SETBACK IS NOT THE END OF THE STORY PUSH YOURSELF TO YOUR NEXT GREAT CHAPTER

For the next few years, I lived in low-income housing while raising my boys and working at Woodward's department store. Then, I left my job at Woodward's and began a career in banking. I started out on the front lines working as a teller. After six weeks I was promoted to the prestigious side counter position. Within a year I was promoted again to managing tens of millions of dollars of lawyers' trust funds in an exclusive, independent position.

I was always pushing myself to be better, to do more, be more, have more so I could give more. I wanted to improve myself and my income to support my family. I had an internal drive to never give up. I wanted to prove everyone wrong. I would make it. I could do this! During these years I learned to appreciate life's lessons and gifts and I continued to grow.

Ten years after my first marriage, I married a second time. I became pregnant soon after our wedding in Hawaii but spent most of my time during our marriage being neglected by my husband. As soon as my daughter was born, I no longer existed in his eyes. I later found out that my husband had a girlfriend before, during, and after our entire marriage. He worked with her; she was married, too, and the four of us occasionally hung out together as couples. Needless to say, the marriage did not last, but I would not change a thing as I have my beautiful daughter from that relationship.

I spent the next years relentlessly trying to find my passion. I worked in banking, direct sales, office supplies, a genealogical search company, and as a sales manager for a roofing distribution company. I also went to night school while working full-time and raising my kids, to get my diploma in International Trade. Additionally, I began a calling card company in Santiago, Chile that I launched at the Canada/Chile Trade Mission in 2003.

OPPORTUNITY KEEPS KNOCKING, SO OPEN THE DOOR!

I was very proud of the calling card company. It was a crazy dream, but I wanted to make it happen. Recognizing a huge opportunity, I wanted to offer an affordable service that we took for granted in Canada. The large telecommunications companies had a very different view on my entry to the marketplace and I was forced out of business when they pressured my distribution channel to drop me. Unfortunately, my venture was short-lived after significant effort and money had been invested. I planned to travel back to Chile to negotiate a deal with another distributor when I was rear-ended in a car accident and suffered severe whiplash, leaving me unable to travel. I had to move on from this company but by this time I knew it was not the end. I knew other opportunities would come my way.

By 2007, I was working for a computer company selling proprietary software and hardware for restaurants. My expertise in sales and customer service had grown significantly by then. I had come a long way from the introverted little Greek girl who thought she was not good enough. With perseverance, training, and a belief in myself I had become a great salesperson.

I loved working with customers and was enjoying my new career when I began having severe migraines regularly. I was also having issues with my sinuses. I thought I probably had a severe sinus infection, but my nose and upper gums were numb, which was troubling.

That August was one big headache, literally. I had eight migraines that month and each one put me down for two to five days. I went to the doctor and had several tests run, including a CT scan. After the CT scan doctors finally determined the cause of my sinus trouble and migraines.

I will never forget that day. The doctor's office called and scheduled me for a 7:00 PM appointment. The doctor came in and told me that I had a brain tumor and that she was very sorry, but she did not know whether it was benign or malignant. She had not consulted a neurologist before meeting with me. I drove home in a state of shock and called my mom to tell her the news.

I learned that I had a meningioma, a benign brain tumor. After an MRI, I learned it measured 3.3 x 3.4 x 4.4 cm, was in my right frontal lobe, and had probably been growing for twenty or thirty years. Only recently had it grown large enough to begin causing migraines, sinus pain, and facial numbness.

Within a month I would be having major brain surgery to remove the tumor. Oddly enough, I was not scared until the day of the surgery, when it really sunk in. I had been told that the tumor was in an excellent location for surgery and that I would not need chemo or radiation afterwards. The tumor was not going to kill me. But with any surgery there is always a risk.

I do not remember much that happened the first week or so post-surgery. When I really came around and began noticing things, the first thing that caught my attention was that I was having significant vision problems. The brain surgeon had touched a nerve in my right eye, causing fourth nerve palsy. I always had this weird talent to do crazy thing with my eyes and move them independently, but this was something I could not control. I had severe double vision. I could only see straight when I looked through a very narrow view if I tilted my chin down. And I could not look to my left at all. When I tried, I lost all focus and control of my eyes.

This condition is similar to a child having a wandering eye. Actually, I had to be seen at Vancouver Children's Hospital to have my condition monitored. This was a very challenging time for me. It was one of the worst times of my life. I had so much stress and anxiety wondering if my vision would be like this forever. My head was permanently disfigured, leaving my self-esteem at an all-time low. My jaw was so stiff from surgery that I could barely open my mouth to eat. I was house-bound, and unable to walk up or down stairs without assistance. I could not read or watch TV to occupy myself because I was constantly dizzy. Every negative thought you could possibly imagine ran through my mind thousands of times each day. I wish I had known then what I know now about keeping a positive mindset, the healing powers of affirmations, an attitude of gratitude, and the law of attraction.

I cannot stress enough how important it is to reach out to family and friends to help you during a medical crisis (or any crisis, for that matter). Having people who love you to support you is so important. Being the independent person that I am, I did not ask for much help. Silly me. Stupid me, actually. I did not want to worry my kids any more than they already were. My mother was such an angel. She lived nearby and prepared meals for us, but for the most part, I was alone in my thoughts in a very dark place.

About five weeks into my recovery, I met someone online. Bored out of my mind, I had gone on a dating site, half-blind, looking for strangers to converse with me. Talk about being desperate! For our first meeting, I rode the bus to downtown Vancouver where we met for a drink. He must have thought I was rather forward on a first date when I grabbed his arm to walk up a few stairs. Little did he know that I grabbed his arm so that I would not fall flat on my face.

We hit it off and developed a relationship. He picked me up every day for several weeks and took me out on his random errands just to get me out of the house. Sometimes we would just hang out. At first, I only told him that I'd had a recent eye surgery. Eventually I told him the extent of the surgery. He was also having some challenges in his life, so it was wonderful to be able to help each other. I cannot tell you what a godsend he was for me. He came into my life exactly when I needed him, and I am forever grateful for what he did for me.

Worried about losing my job, I returned to work twelve weeks post-surgery. I was worried about paying my bills and the mortgage on the house I had recently purchased. I needed the money, or so I thought. In hindsight, that was the worst decision I could have made. I suffered with migraines and vision issues for several weeks before the universe decided I'd had enough. All of the senior managers, including me, were laid off from our jobs. It was the biggest blessing.

I did not work for two years. It was a very trying time. The line of credit was on a steady increase as the months went by, but I needed to heal. My vision took over a year to somewhat normalize, and the severe numbness in my face post surgery lasted for several years.

During this period, I had a lot of time to think. My surgery was a life-changing experience. I could have died. I decided to take on a totally different view on life from this time forward. From this point on, any time an opportunity presented itself I was going to take it.

DEFINE YOUR WORK AND WHAT YOU NEED

Knowing that after all my health problems I would need a job that allowed me to make my health a priority, I decided to choose a job that would work for me rather than choosing to work for the job. I started slowly by taking a 100% sales commission, part-time position that allowed me to work as much or as little as I wanted.

I told my bosses about my medical condition, and that I was not sure how I would respond to being back to work. My boss told me that as long as I was meeting or exceeding my quotas that he would not micromanage me. I would be allowed to do my own thing, which was perfect for me. For some this would be a scary venture to undertake, but I was up for the challenge.

I pushed myself by working long hours, often answering customer emails at 6:00 AM before I went to work and again well into the evening. I needed to build up my customer base and wanted to ensure they were well taken care of. Within less than six months I was working full-time and making a full-time income. I was back!

After working for this company for about four years, a couple of millennials were hired into the mix, and that changed everything for me. I was working independently with little interaction with my bosses for the most part and the millennials were cc'ing him on every email they sent. This is when my interest in generational differences in the workplace was first piqued.

Although I enjoyed the work and my co-workers, my bosses were a different story. My work environment left much to be desired. Receiving year-end bonuses based on sales is a standard practice in the world of sales. When I did not receive a bonus at the end of 2013 because my boss said I was "already making too much money," I decided to look at other business opportunities. Forever the entrepreneur!

I continued working my sales job while seeking other opportunities. I joined an Australian direct sales company and quickly rose to the top of their company, becoming one of their top 20 earners out of 20,000 consultants. I had 1,700 consultants on my team and was the only director in North America. I earned free trips to Australia, Dubai, Aruba, Florence, Manchester, Dallas, and Los Angeles. I finally left my sales job in 2016 to pursue my new business venture full-time.

DREAM BIG AND HELP OTHERS DREAM TOO

I LOVED working with my team. Coaching and mentoring were my passion. In October 2016, I attended a One Day to Greatness seminar with Jack Canfield in Kamloops, BC. After a brief conversation with Jack, I decided to take his Train the Trainer course to become a certified Success Principles Trainer. The intention was to share this new knowledge with my team. I had found purpose and passion in supporting others to build successful teams. I felt fulfilled when I saw their self-esteem and confidence grow. They were conquering their fears and winning!

Unfortunately, I had to resign from the direct sales company in February 2017 when they started having issues with production and delivery. Later that year the company declared bankruptcy. I went through a lot of stress, anxiety, and loss of sleep. Panic attacks became the daily norm for me. I had known the CEO for over eighteen years and was completely in the dark about the state of the company. My team was upset and blaming me. I received a constant stream of Facebook messages and harassing emails. The downfall of the company was out of my control, so I had to bow out. But this was not my first time at the rodeo. I knew that my story did not stop here if I chose to keep trying.

I met someone in late 2016 who introduced me to an opportunity to speak and train businesses on generational differences in the workplace. I was fascinated by this as I saw the struggles my own millennial children were having at work. I look back now at the communication challenges that existed in my previous jobs and wish I knew then how the different generations think and process information. I wanted to more closely understand their environment and what I could do to help. It made perfect sense that bridging the generation gap would improve productivity, communication, collaboration, and make for a happier, more cohesive work environment.

I now know that the behaviors, attitudes, beliefs, experiences, and influences during an individual's formative years really shape who they are and how they behave in all areas of their lives. I was excited about my new-found knowledge, and planned to launch my speaking business by mid-2017.

I hired an image consultant to come to my home and do a complete wardrobe change to prepare me for my speaking career. Having someone go through my wardrobe and tell me to get rid of most of it was a very difficult experience. There were a few tears. I must have attachment issues! I eventually embraced the change and spent thousands of dollars on a new wardrobe to complete my new look.

Then, as luck would have it, I broke a veneer on my front tooth. No big deal, I thought. I had been through this before and would just have it replaced.

This was the beginning of my dental nightmare. From May 31, 2017 through December 21, 2017, I had twenty-six dental appointments to fix my front tooth. I began lisping and developed what doctors believe is a stress-related condition. I lost the saliva in my mouth, had burning in my throat from acid reflux brought on by stress, my voice was constantly hoarse, and I spent several months waking up with panic attacks. I never knew from one to day to the next if I would have a voice or not, so I had to put everything on hold.

I saw every doctor and specialist I believed might be able to help me. I was taking six pills a day to help with my various symptoms. I hated this! I needed to feel better; I needed to heal my body naturally. I would not stop until I got the answers I needed. I moved away from traditional medicine, stopped taking all my medications, and began incorporating EFT (Emotional Freedom Technique), also known as Tapping, Reiki, and Bioenergy work, to heal my body.

Eventually, my body and voice were getting to the point where I could speak relatively well, I decided to move forward with the training business. I hired a business coach to get me on the right track, mentally and physically. He helped me tremendously during a very difficult time. I also attended Raymond Aaron's Speaker and Communication Workshop, which totally changed my training and speaking style. It gave me the confidence I was lacking and sent me on a whole new trajectory for my business. I began my own company, Gen-Connect Training in early 2018. It has been an amazing ride. I am much more at peace and ready for the next stage in my life.

LIVING IN THE POSITIVE HAS MADE MY LIFE

Although I have been blessed with many struggles, I have also enjoyed many successes. I have experienced relationships that did not work out, work and business challenges, worries when raising three children as a single parent, medical challenges, and many dreams and goals that seemed impossible. The one thing I always knew for sure was that if I gave up and wallowed in self-pity, I would be letting myself and my children down. That was not an option. Success was the only acceptable outcome.

I wanted to show my children what a strong, self-sufficient and resourceful mother I could be, and that they could always rely on me. I wanted to set an example and prove to myself and my children that I could provide for us no matter what. I am very proud of the amazing people my children have become; they are strong, independent, kind, respectful, and loving. This is the true meaning of success for me. Out of all the things I have accomplished thus far, they are my crowning glory.

FIVE STRATEGIES FOR A SUCCESSFUL LIFE

1) Always have a positive mindset. This is a crucial component. Before you get into the power of a positive mindset and the law of attraction, spend some time listening to what you are currently telling yourself. Check in with yourself. What is going on with you? We constantly speak to ourselves with an inner voice which is sometimes quietly whispering and sometimes yelling. Once you have spent a few days noticing how you speak to yourself, you may not like it very much; after all, you are your own worst critic. Be accountable for how you speak to yourself. Never fear, you have the power to change that inner voice!

Do you believe you are the product of everything that has happened to you in your life? Your inner voice may try to convince you that you are a victim of your circumstances and your past. Reflect and acknowledge the things that have happened to you and where you are now. Then prepare to move past them.

2) Shift your mindset using the law of attraction. You can influence things around you so that things happen FOR you rather than TO you. The universal principle of the law of attraction is that 'like attracts like.' The law of attraction manifests through your thoughts by drawing to you not only thoughts and ideas that are alike, but also people who think like you, along with corresponding situations and possibilities. It is the magnetic power of the universe which draws similar energies to each other.

The law of attraction is already working in your life, intentional or not. If you have a negative mindset, many unpleasant or unwanted things are probably happening in your life, and you may see negative things happening all around you. Think back to how you speak to yourself. Be mindful of your thoughts and that inner voice. Begin to think positively.

Along with thinking positively, begin to intentionally think and feel the things that you would like to have in your life. The most common things people desire are love, a career, good relationships, health, and wealth. Visualize a mental image of what you want to achieve. Repeat positive, affirming statements to create and bring into your life what you visualize or repeat in your mind. In other words, use the power of your thoughts and words.

Imagine that what you desire is already a part of your life. Acknowledge it with each of your five senses, to the extent that you can. Spend time imagining your life once you have acquired what it is that you want. Write out your affirmations and read them aloud at least once daily. You will begin to draw them to you when you act as though you already have what it is that you want. Persistence is key!

3) Take calculated risks. Do you encourage yourself to stay where you are and play it safe? Safe can be dangerous. I encourage you to take calculated risks. If you do not try new things you will never know how far you can go. When opportunities present themselves, jump on them. It may be your one and only chance. Push yourself and do not take no for an answer. Keep digging until you find the answer you want.

Quitting is always an option. Well, it is an option for those who are content living a mediocre life. Quitting is an option unless you want to live an amazing life with a purpose. If you want to live the life of your dreams, you must not give up. Do not give up and never stop learning. If you continue to learn, you will continue to grow both personally and professionally.

4) Appreciate all of life's lessons and gifts with an attitude of gratitude. Learn and grow from your failures. Let life's challenges teach you to persevere even when all you want to do is give up. Remind yourself that the only outcome you will accept is success.

5) NEVER Give Up. We all face adversities and challenges in life. It takes character, drive, and a positive mindset to persevere, overcome, and excel in life. The only person who can stop you from achieving your goals is you. If I can do it, so can you. Go for it!

Do you, your team, or organization want to be inspired to change your future and find your purpose?

Do you want to learn how mastering the Five Strategies for A Success Life can empower you in both your personal and professional career?

Do you want to say "NO TO THE PITY PARTY" and achieve the life you truly desire?

Vivian Stark is an inspirational speaker and corporate trainer living in Vancouver, B.C. Canada, whose captivating story will inspire you to live the life you want if you never, never, never give up on what's important – You.

As a generational and workplace effectiveness expert, Vivian's career centers around helping others work in a more collaborative and cohesive work environment. Her focus on engagement and accountability both in and outside of the workplace mirrors her personal belief of how you must take 100% responsibility in all areas of your life. Learn how giving up blaming, complaining and excuse making can lead you to live a life filled with peace, happiness and personal fulfillment.

To learn how you can incorporate her knowledge and expertise into your life and business with ease and confidence, reach out to Vivian at www.gen-connect.ca. Vivian is available for private or corporate speaking engagements.

Your Life Energy

AMAL INDI

I have 20 years of experience in the tech sector and corporate banking. In my previous life in the "Rat Race", I was waking up every day and going to a job that provided well for me. After some major changes in my life (including a divorce), I started recognizing that I wasn't intrinsically happy. I would be going about my day filled with negative thoughts and emotions. It felt as though they were taking over in a way, and I recognized how they were beginning to affect every moment of my day and every interaction with those around me. I refer to these as "Thought Bugs", which I will go on to explain later. These Thought Bugs were almost like a computer virus, affecting all the thoughts or, as one may say, programming in my mind. After recognizing these Bugs and studying them in myself for many years, I began to draw strong conclusions about how I could create positive change in my mind. This positive change in my thoughts would eventually lead to me leaving the "Rat Race" and starting on the mission of my life to share my new paradigm with those around me. I believe that we can change our minds and create a positive and uplifting life, not only for ourselves, but for those around us. I would love to share with you the basics of what I discovered, a new way of examining our thought patterns and how to drastically shift the energy around you (your Aura) so that you can lead a fantastic life!

GETTING STARTED ON YOUR OWN JOURNEY

When was the last time you really felt 100%? When I say 100%, I mean you wake up feeling a general positivity in your mood, you are looking forward to a new day, your interactions with people feel good, and you walk around feeling a general sense of purpose even with the simple tasks of getting groceries or whatever your work environment. You may think that you have no say in how you really feel. That deep down, you cannot control your thoughts and emotions. I know that this is not true. I developed a unique way of seeing our minds and how deeply they affect our energy. Have you heard of life energy, such as positive energy, negative energy, Aura energy, and universal energy? Read on!

WHAT MAKES US HUMAN?

Each one of us is a biological marvel of different cells, tissues, genes. These are the many working pieces that come together to create our human body. What really makes us human in a whole sense? We each possess an in-depth energetic landscape that we can't deny. This energetic pulse is used by scientists and technicians daily to perform tests and create pictures of our bodies and their functions. Think of the neuroscientists that connect our bodies to electrodes and measure our brain waves. That's part of it. We can't deny there is a part of us beyond just the tissues of our muscles and bones.

Did you know that surrounding you right now is an energy field that is all your own? This energetic field is referred to as your Aura. This Aura can be the beginning of a life that you love. Every human being has an energy field around them. We cannot see this field with the naked eye. However, we can see this field with an Aura machine. It's true! I personally have had mine captured and what was reflected back to me (in terms of energetic levels) was what I was truly feeling.

Your Aura and the energy you radiate is 100% in your control. Some days, you might feel positive and good, while other days, you may feel more negative and lower. These are your energy levels. They can vibrate high or low. It depends on you and your thoughts. Remember, with improvements to your mind and thoughts, your aura energy field will continuously change, thus altering the life you are leading.

YOUR AURA

Over the centuries of humans existing and contemplating our existence, many have acknowledged the fact that we have an energy that extends beyond our skin and flesh, which can actually interact with the world around us. This is referred to as your body's Aura. The Aura refers to the energy around your body that can be affected from the inside out or the outside in. When it is strong, the Aura around your body can extend quite a way beyond the barrier of your physical body (your skin). It can also manifest as different colours, depending on the emotional mood of the person. For example, when you are in a state of calm, then you will exude a white Aura. When you are in a state of anger, then you will exude a red Aura. Sometimes Auras may also be a combination of different colours. There is technology now that can show the colour and strength of someone's Aura. I have had mine checked. One day, it was light in colour and extended far beyond my body. This didn't surprise me as I feel I live in a state of calm, clear energy and my inner emotional landscape is positive. If you were to have an opportunity to get yours checked today what do you think the results would be? Strong and white? Or weak and maybe red? Maybe you feel like it may not show up at all.

This is what I want to teach you. This is my mission right now: To help you understand that you can empower yourself and create a strong, positive Aura that will not only affect your overall sense of well-being. It will affect your relationships, your business, and your life as a whole.

YOUR HUMAN SYSTEM

Through my own exploration, I began seeing and noticing a pattern in how my Aura was being affected by different things in my life. As I continued to study this in myself, it became clear to me that that there were specific things in play, and it was all rooted in my mind. Having a strong background in technology, I began to clearly see how our own minds behave like supercomputers. (Stay with me here!) Just like a super computer, we have our own operating system and the ability to run many programs at once. We are constantly juggling responsibilities, taking in the world around us, assessing how we feel, and determining what we need. The list could go on and on! Just take a moment right now: close your eyes and connect to all the "programs" open in your mind that are constantly running. Relate that to being connected to your own unique operating system of your mind. Now imagine that a computer virus was implanted into one of your programs and began affecting your thoughts. Computer viruses are designed to spread to all parts of a computer with the goal of eventually changing the computer, more often than not, making it completely dysfunctional. This is what can happen in your mind. A negative thought may enter your mind about something specific. Maybe a co-worker engages you in conversation about a rumour that someone is up for raise (one that you applied for) or on your coffee break the barista makes a mistake on your order and you feel it ruins your morning. I call these viruses of our thoughts Human Errors. In its most basic form, Human Errors can be outlined as the following emotions, or what I like to call Thought Bugs:

- Anger
- Suspicion
- Craving
- Comparison
- Low self-esteem
- Procrastination
- Getting stuck in negative thoughts

What it can be boiled down to is that these negative thought bugs can enter into your mind, which in turn creates negative energy. This leads to stress and a weakening of your Aura.

I'm sure you can think of a definitive moment, probably even within the last day or the last week, where you can see how your own errors were affecting your core system and negatively impacting the energy around you.

Luckily, we have a set of more positive emotions and various ways of reacting that counter the negative ones. I have identified these and aptly named them our Human Features.

Primary Human features that combat the errors include:

- Love and kindness
- Acceptance
- Forgiveness
- Courageousness
- Patience
- Authenticity
- Gratefulness

One can think of these features as a built-in tool box to combat negativity. This is always at our disposal! I want to help you identify where these positive emotions are in you, so that you may have access them and strengthen the energy that you are putting out into the world and your Aura.

Look, I am not a psychologist. I am not a therapist. I am, however, a believer in how we show up to our work and interact with those around us will have a deep impact on the life we are creating for ourselves. I have firsthand experience. I have taken myself from a place of negativity and darkness to a place of possibility. I have watched my newfound passions and work flourish, along with my relationships, personal and otherwise.

This is a different way of looking at things. This just isn't your usual "Be positive" message. This is connecting into the fact that as humans, we have a distinct design in place to help us truly create a good life for ourselves. The foundation of this is to truly feel happy and positive from the inside out, so that what we engage with is affected by our positive energy. Think of the last time you had an encounter with someone who you felt emitted a positive or happy energy? How did it make you feel? How did you react? You truly have the power to combat these negative thought processes (bugs) already in you! Don't you want to be the one truly living in your potential and sharing your positivity with everyone and everything in your life?

THE "AWESOME LIFE" IS WAITING FOR YOU!

Let's get down to business. Thanks for sticking with me. If you have continued reading to this point, then I want to applaud you! It means that you are deeply interested in living your best life.

Side effects of a mind free from negative Thought Bugs may include:
- General feelings of happiness and relaxation
- Genuine connections when meeting people
- A mind free from clutter
- A deep appreciation for the world and people around you
- High levels of productivity
- Willingness to learn new skills
- Gaining more contacts and connections with ease
- Feeling an authentic excitement for projects and self-development
- Being ready to rock your life!

These are just a few of the feelings available to you if you commit to removing negative Thought Bugs from your life, thus strengthening your energy and Aura from the inside out. I wouldn't be here today if I didn't do the work and experience the benefits of being on the other side of the process.

BRING LIGHT TO YOU

My hope for you is to learn how to identify your negative Thought Bugs and stop their process of multiplication. For you to empower yourself with positivity and strengthen your aura. For you to leave feelings of depletion behind and bring your energy back to 100%. For you to share your positive energy with the world and make it a better place!

Never forget: An Awesome Life is within your reach at all times. I believe it. In fact, I will go so far as to say I know it is. I have taken my own life and made it awesome by taking all I have outlined in my work and applying it to myself. Now it is your turn to turn up the positivity in your life and let your Aura shine!

I encourage you to check out my website, www.happinessmountain.com, to receive a free guide on removing your negative energy. In this guide, you will also be given a sneak peek into the app I am developing. The Happiness Mountain™ app will quickly become your new best friend! I developed the Happiness Mountain™ app to be a way to actually track those negative Thought Bugs and coach you to clear your worries and boost your energy levels! By giving you this important tool at your fingertips, I know you will be able to strengthen your energy and basically start living a more happy life! If you haven't guessed already, I love technology and its possibilities for enhancing our lives. I can't wait for you to be one of the first people to try this app and reap its benefits right away at www.happinessmountain.com/app.

BRINGING LIGHT TO YOU SO THAT YOU MAY BRING LIGHT TO THE WORLD

Now that I have given you some insight on how you can truly change your life by changing your own energy, I want to share the ways that Happiness Mountain™ can help you begin to apply these concepts. The process of understanding, application, and execution is key when committing to changing the way your mind functions and, over time, changing your aura.

Now that you know you have the power to change your life via your thoughts, I wonder why you wouldn't want to act now to change your life. Your own personal idea of an awesome life is within reach! I left behind an old way of living and being in order to start on a new path. I am confident that you have the power to do that for yourself as well. We all just need a little help. To be honest, I wish I had connected with these deeper levels of understanding regarding my thoughts and how they affect my life earlier. However, as we all know, timing is everything, especially when it comes to your advancement on both a personal level and a business one. Take this as a sign that it may be time for you to dive into these deep changes. The techniques, once you really begin to understand them, are quite straightforward. I know that you live a busy life and are striving to do your best. However, it takes commitment to change. Why not start now?

Happiness Mountain™ can offer you many tools to get started and help you dive deeper. The first step is easy! I encourage you to head over to my website www.happinessmountain.com to sign up and stay connected to the developments in my work. You will automatically receive an easy to follow guide on how to remove your negative energy, which will be delivered right to your inbox! You will also be given an automatic sneak peek into my app.

THE HAPPINESS MOUNTAIN™ APP

I am constantly inspired by how we connect online through different platforms and technologies. I believe that this can be the start to a great change in how we grow and develop. I designed the app as a convenient way for you to connect to your energy boosting practices on the go. We all spend some time on our phones scrolling and engaging on different platforms. Why not invest that time mindfully instead of mindlessly? The Happiness Mountain™ app, www.happinessmountain.com/app, helps you do that by having the tools you can utilize to boost your own positive energy available at any time!

Features include the following:

- Troubleshooting what is worrying you and replacing that worry with positivity

- Ways to resolve disputes without creating negative energy and affecting your Aura

- Aura boosting activities you can do on daily basis, while tracking your progress with your own private point system

- An emergency toolkit for handling sudden negative situations

- An easy guide to all the Thought Bugs and how to handle them available at a touch of your screen, so that you may continue to learn how you can change your thoughts to more positive ones and keep your positive energy high!

HAPPINESS MOUNTAIN™ FOR KIDS

Calling all parents and anyone who takes care of children! This work isn't just applicable to more mature minds and bodies. It can start when we are young! I am in the process of finishing development on a series of books for children that will cover all the core concepts of my work and Happiness Mountain™, so that we may share these valuable tools and concepts even with the developing minds of the next generation. Of course, there will be interactive games for children as well, because as we all know that some of the best learning happens when we are having fun! This goes for adults too, don't you think? Stay in the loop by connecting with me at www.happinessmountain.com.

MY NEXT BOOK

I am ready to dive deeper and share with you even more in my new book, *Happiness Mountain™: Double Your Happiness, Awesomeness and Spirituality*. In the book we are going to explore deeper than ever before. *Happiness Mountain™* will go more in depth on how you can harness the three levels of energy (Positive/Negative, Aura and Universal) to change your perspective and unlock your perfect life. I want to share with you the techniques and deep processes that will affect all aspects of your life. Remember those 'Negative Thought Bugs' I was talking about earlier? In my new book I will teach you not only how to eliminate them, I want to teach you how to protect yourself from future encounters with 'Negative Thought Bugs' therefore truly creating change in your life for the better. You will also learn techniques on how to recharge your energy, boost your aura and use your new skills for resolving conflicts and affecting your business.

I want you to harness the power of your personal Positive & Aura energies, learn to dance with the Universal energy that is always at your disposable and be able to live at a level of existence that falls in line with your ideal, perfect life. Take a look at the *Happiness Mountain™* diagram on the next page. You can define your perfect life as living with a high level of inner peace, the level of inner happiness. Your Awesome Life and Spiritual Life revolves around being of service to others and helping others. You can live a combination of all levels of the *Happiness Mountain™*. Whatever you personally define as perfection is where you have the power.

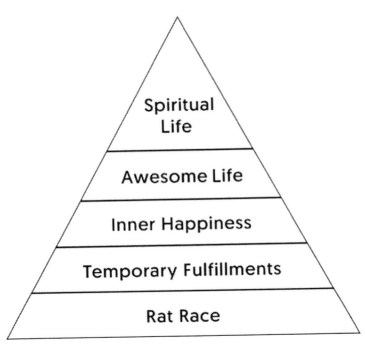

Happiness Mountain™ created by Amal Indi

Some might argue you cannot have a perfect life. I say you already have a perfect life and it is blocked by negative energy from coming into full fruition. This negative energy can be existing as a low self-esteem bug or a comparison bug. You may define perfect life as comparing to others. You may try to achieve things with craving energy. Please remember: You are already whole, complete and perfect. You cannot access your full power because of the negative energy being generated by your thoughts. When you learn to remove those negative thoughts as I teach you in *Happiness Mountain™*, you will realize how much power you have in life. This will be your turning point to harness the energy to power-up your personal, business and spiritual life! In the book I will give you all the tools and techniques to accomplish that. After reading my new book *Happiness Mountain™* you will be able to shift your life to a new paradigm that is not only accessible but exciting. How do you think it will feel to lead a perfect life? Can you think of even one thing that may change for the better if you decided to investigate how you could crush your negative energies, enhance your positive energies and essentially eliminate future worries from your life? … Wow! I am excited for you just thinking about it myself! I know the profound changes it created for me in my life and I look forward to hearing how it affects yours.

YOU CAN LEAD AN AWESOME LIFE

My hope for you is to learn how to identify your negative Thought Bugs and stop their process of multiplication. For you to empower yourself with positivity and strengthen your aura. For you to leave feelings of depletion behind and bring your energy back to 100%. For you to share your positive energy with the world and make it a better place!

Never forget: The Awesome Life is within your reach at all times. I believe it. In fact, I will go as so far to say I know it is. I have taken my own life and made it perfect in my eyes by taking all I have outlined in my work and applying it to myself. Again, your negative thoughts may say your life is not perfect, which might include your low self-esteem, cravings, or comparison bugs blocking you. Don't let these bugs create negative energy. Instead, clear them and power-up the personal, business, or spiritual aspects of your life. Never forget you have the power over your own mind- NOT your negative Thought Bugs. Now it is time to power-up the positivity in your life and let your Aura shine!

I encourage you to check out my website, www.happinessmountain.com, for the opportunity to stay connected to the global community of people who have already begun to use this work to boost their positivity and create their

Awesome Life in their personal, business, and spiritual domains. I can't wait for you to begin using The Happiness Mountain™ App to start training your energy to stay positive and even get stronger. Of course, I encourage you to visit www.happinessmountain.com to stay connected and be in the know as to what is coming down the pipeline with this life changing work.

I have dedicated my life to bringing these concepts and work to you. I know you can change your energy and begin to not only affect your own life, but the entire world. I believe deeply that when as many people as possible align their energy to a higher, more positive state, then we can truly make a collective difference. Let's start today!

Amal Indi lives in Vancouver, Canada, and is the founder and CEO of Happiness Mountain™ Inc. After 20 years of working in technology and corporate banking, Amal is on a mission to give people the possibility to live with their full potential in their personal, business, and spiritual domains. He has found innovative techniques and tools to remove negative energy and power up your personal life, business life, and spiritual life. Ultimately, you can make the world a more awesome place for everyone. He believes that technology has the potential to transform the minds and energy of people and facilitate change. Amal wants to help people around the globe live a positive and enriching life through the energy-based tools and techniques of this innovative system he has developed to strengthen your energy and help you live a life full of happiness and potential. Find his story and work at www.happinessmountain.com.